Prayer
in the
Making

The Bible Reading Fellowship
15 The Chambers, Vineyard
Abingdon OX14 3FE
brf.org.uk

The Bible Reading Fellowship (BRF) is a Registered Charity (233280)

ISBN 978 0 85746 801 7
First published 2019
10 9 8 7 6 5 4 3 2 1 0
All rights reserved

Acknowledgements
Unless otherwise acknowledged, scripture quotations are taken from the Holy Bible, New
International Version (Anglicised edition) copyright © 1979, 1984, 2011 by Biblica. Used by
permission of Hodder & Stoughton Publishers, a Hachette UK company. All rights reserved. 'NIV' is
a registered trademark of Biblica. UK trademark number 1448790.

Scripture quotations marked 'MSG' are taken from *The Message*, copyright © 1993, 1994, 1995,
1996, 2000, 2001, 2002 by Eugene H. Peterson. Used by permission of NavPress. All rights reserved.
Represented by Tyndale House Publishers, Inc.

Scripture quotations marked 'TPT' are taken from The Passion Translation. Copyright © 2017 by
Passion & Fire Ministries, Inc. Used by permission. All rights reserved. **thePassionTranslation.com**

Scripture quotations marked 'NLT' are taken from the Holy Bible, New Living Translation,
copyright © 1996, 2004, 2007, 2013. Used by permission of Tyndale House Publishers, Inc.,
Carol Stream, Illinois 60188. All rights reserved.

Scripture quotations marked 'ESV' are taken from the Holy Bible, English Standard Version,
published by HarperCollins Publishers, © 2001 Crossway Bibles, a division of Good News
Publishers. Used by permission. All rights reserved.

Scripture quotations marked 'NASB' are taken from the New American Standard Bible, copyright
© 1960, 1962, 1963, 1968, 1971, 1972, 1973, 1975, 1977, 1995 by The Lockman Foundation. Used by
permission. **Lockman.org**

Scripture quotations marked 'AMP' are taken from the Amplified Bible (AMP), copyright © 2015 by
The Lockman Foundation. Used by permission. **Lockman.org**

Every effort has been made to trace and contact copyright owners for material used in this
resource. We apologise for any inadvertent omissions or errors, and would ask those concerned
to contact us so that full acknowledgement can be made in the future.

A catalogue record for this book is available from the British Library

Printed and bound by CPI Group (UK) Ltd, Croydon CR0 4YY

Prayer in the Making

Trying it, talking it, sustaining it

Lyndall Bywater

Foreword by Roy Searle

Contents

Foreword

If you are hesitant or put off by books on prayer, this isn't one of them. If you're looking for a weighty treatise on the subject of prayer, this is not the book for you. But if you're looking for a practical and encouraging book on how we might pray, this book will be very helpful. It's clearly written by someone who both prays and encourages and facilitates others to pray.

In this follow-up book to her *Faith in the Making*, Lyndall inspires, enlightens and encourages readers to engage with prayer not out of obligation or a sense of guilt or duty, but in response to following Jesus and to a deepening relationship with him and the world.

Thank God there is no claim here to some special revelation, new wave, latest trend or a one-size-fits-all mentality. Rather, this book is a carefully considered and helpful guide to prayer. Like the best guidebooks, *Prayer in the Making* is an excellent travelling companion for those who want to journey in prayer. Lyndall takes us on a tour of twelve different types of prayer, with each one linked to a different scripture or biblical character. We journey through the experiences of encounter, worship, listening, stillness, action, intercession, strategy, restoration, voice and body, scripture, warfare and resilience. Each chapter explores its theme, drawing from scripture and the wisdom and experience gleaned from other sources.

Lyndall writes poignantly from her own personal experience and explores the issues relating to prayer from various angles and perspectives. She introduces us to different streams of spirituality and methods of prayer, old and new, and she explores the relationship between prayer and our personalities and persuasions.

The aim of the book is clear: to build a sustainable, life-giving rhythm of prayer. As the title suggests, there are ingredients and elements that need to be explored and experienced in shaping a life of prayer, and each chapter helpfully includes explanations and examples, as well as a practical section that encourages the reader to try it and sustain it.

Prayer in the Making is accessible, down-to-earth, insightful and inspiring. Journey with it as a companion and find its teaching, suggestions and activities an invaluable resource to a deeper, more intentional, life of prayer.

Roy Searle, leader of Northumbria Community, former president of the Baptist Union of Great Britain, tutor at Cranmer Hall, Durham, and member of the Renovare Board

Introduction

I was a student in my first year at university when I had my first brush with a cult. I had just navigated past that awkward bit where you try to work out whether you're friends with Jesus because your parents told you that it was a good idea or because it really is a good idea. I had decided it was, and I was passionate about my new-found 'adult' faith. So when a lady sat down near me in the college refectory and invited some other girls to a Bible study, I had no qualms about interrupting their conversation and asking if she'd like to come and study the Bible with me, too.

It only took two of those Bible studies for my fragile, not-so-grown-up faith to be blown apart. In two weeks, I went from zealous believing to anxious doubting. I felt as though a very important rug had been pulled out from under my feet, and I wasn't sure I could even call myself a Christian, given how far my life had apparently strayed from the 'right' path. It was then that I discovered one of the best reasons for finding Christian friends at university. I explained my dilemma to another member of the Christian Union, and she offered to join me at the next Bible study.

The study ran its usual course, with the lady explaining to us both why we were probably failing to meet the mark on a number of matters pertaining to life and godliness, and then she suddenly threw in a killer question: 'When you get up in the morning, how do you decide who you are going to evangelise to?'

Well, I was horrified. I might once have been a keen Jesus-follower – before the great dismantling had occurred – but I'd never been that keen on evangelism, and I certainly didn't do it every day. As I floundered in yet more guilt, my friend uttered one simple phrase that entirely revolutionised not only the course of those Bible studies, but indeed the course of my whole life. She simply said, 'I ask God who he wants me to talk to about Jesus, and he tells me.'

The temperature of the conversation suddenly dropped by several degrees. New shadows of suspicion darkened the lady's tone as she asked, 'You hear God speaking?'

'Yes, of course. I talk to him and he talks to me,' said my friend.

'Through the Bible, of course…'

'Yes, through the Bible, but he speaks directly to me by his Holy Spirit, too. I hear his voice in my mind.'

The lady seemed stunned into horrified silence. Picking up her bag, she walked out of my room and I never saw her again. Perhaps that little snippet of conversation was enough to persuade her that my friend was beyond hope – and that I was, too, by association – but I can't help hoping that it lodged with her in some way, and that she has since found the truth of my friend's words for herself: that we have a God who can speak, who does speak and who loves to communicate directly with us, his beloved.

It may well have been that day that I fell in love with prayer. Christianity comes alive for all of us in different ways, but for me it was that realisation that to follow Jesus is to be part of a conversation. Suddenly I knew again that I was loved, that I was welcome and that I wasn't doing such a terrible job of being a Christian after all. If it's about talking and listening, then I reckoned I could manage that.

Prayer is simultaneously the simplest and the most complex thing I know in life. At its simplest, it is what my friend described: it is us talking to God and him talking to us. Yet it is also the story of tiny, insubstantial human beings communicating with one who exists outside of time and beyond eternity. It's as simple as the world's most basic transistor radio picking up radio waves, but it's as complex as that same little transistor radio somehow tuning into the echoes of distant stars. If you think about it too much, it can make your brain fizz.

Prayer is a wonder, in every sense of the word. It is unfathomable and beautiful and joyfully real. The God we worship has always spoken, right from the very conception of creation, and he hasn't stopped. Jesus, God made man, spent the vast majority of his ministry talking and listening. He wasn't a guru who poked his head out of a cave every six months or so to utter something profound; he was the man who told stories and chatted at parties. When he was getting ready to face the cross, he told his followers what it would be like to have him around in spirit instead of in person, and the Spirit he described was a distinctly talkative one: one who would teach and tell and proclaim; one who would even hear us and communicate with us when we don't have the words anymore. Our God is ever and always in conversation with us, if we want him to be.

Some years ago, I worked for The Salvation Army as National Prayer Coordinator. The job took me all over the country, teaching and preaching on prayer, and I absolutely loved it. I was only a few months into the job when I began to discover a phenomenon that will be familiar to anyone who has ever taught on prayer. I call it the 'guilty prayer slump'. Picture the scene: you stand up in front of an eager congregation, all expectant for the deep wisdoms that the visiting speaker has come to share, and you utter the immortal words, 'Today I'm going to talk about prayer.'

In the heartbeat that follows, something in the room seems to shift. Shoulders sag, heads bow in mild embarrassment and you might even hear a few awkward coughs. I remember getting rather distressed the first few times it happened, but mercifully it didn't take me long to realise that this was no reflection on me; this was a common and widespread reaction to the idea of a talk on prayer. Mention that prayer is the chosen subject for the day, and suddenly a maelstrom of guilt surges through the average congregation of faithful, dedicated Christians. It's not that we don't love prayer. Like me in those early university days, most people love the idea of that simple, two-way communication with a living God. It's just that we're sure we're not doing it properly.

Fast-forward to the coffee slot after the church service, and I would stand there with my cup of tea, looking forward to some inspiring conversations about prayer, only to find myself talking to person after person who wanted me to know how bad they were at it. Some 20 years on, I still have no idea what 'bad at prayer' actually means, but I have found one common denominator in all those conversations. When I ask people to tell me what they think their prayer life should be like, they all refer me to someone else's. It might be a hero of the faith, like John Wesley or Smith Wigglesworth, or it might be someone else in their church or family – a grandmother who prayed for several hours a day or a pastor who told stories of powerful encounters with God in his book-lined study. As they lamented their poor performance, there would always be a litany of comparisons. At the heart of most people's guilt over prayer is the profound belief that others are doing it better than they are.

In the days before his death, one of Jesus' strongest messages to his disciples was about the importance of them being themselves. In John 15, his words have a kind of refrain running through them based around the idea of remaining. They were to remain in him and he would remain in them. He had no designs on becoming some distant deity, and he didn't need them to become spiritual superheroes. He just intended to be right there, with them and in them, by his Spirit.

You only have to read a few chapters of the gospels to know that Jesus mixed with a huge variety of people. His best friends were fishermen, but he could hold his own with the religious academics of his day, and he was completely at ease with the smallest child perched on his knee. We can justifiably conclude that he was a friendly, approachable man, but we can also conclude that he loved human beings – all sorts of human beings. History is full of holy men and women who gathered around them all the 'right' sort of people – people who fitted a certain mould, people who proved to be the best advert for their teachings – but Jesus was shockingly inclusive. His followers weren't a slick set of beautifully homogenised mannequins, all displaying his brand; they were a disparate bunch of folk who probably wouldn't even have interacted with each other if it weren't for their love of the man who had the words of eternal life. Tradesmen mixed with tax collectors; aristocrats ate with one-time lepers; women and foreigners were included and honoured; and the whole colourful lot found themselves embraced in this new kingdom Jesus spoke of.

In fact, the only thing that got you disbarred was hypocrisy – that terrible art of pretending to be something you're not. To him it mattered not one iota how flawed people were, so long as they were honest about their shortcomings and willing to learn. The one person Jesus apparently couldn't work with was someone who had already decided they needed to fake it, pretending to be something they weren't.

The way we're each made is no coincidence. We are the work of a master artisan who has never made a mistake in his life. We are as varied as snowflakes and as complex as stars. He has no desire to make us all the same, but he does long to be in close, intimate relationship with each one of us. That leads me to conclude that his relationship with each one of us must look completely different. No one in all of history will ever reflect God's beauty in quite the same way you do, and no one will ever have the same relationship with him that you have. So, if you buy the lie that you need to become someone else, someone better, in order to be close to him, then that precious, once-in-an-eternity friendship never gets off the ground. You miss out on him, because 'faking it' will always sour the connection; and he misses out because no one can ever be you quite as well as you can.

And if your relationship with him is unique, then so is your prayer life. Your communication with him has a flavour unlike anyone else's. Perhaps you bemoan how feeble and faithless your prayers seem, but to him they are exquisite.

When I was a child, I used to imagine heaven as a mighty sorting office of prayers. I would see prayers drift in like tiny fragments of paper, and then a host of dedicated angels would read each one, digest its contents and sort it to the most appropriate drawer in the filing cabinet, to be processed by the Almighty at his convenience.

One day, my lovely, tidy scene got thoroughly trashed. Suddenly the little fragments of prayers weren't paper any more; they were tiny, brightly coloured butterflies, and they were everywhere! Try as they might, the angels couldn't get a single one of them to stay still long enough to see what it was about. The whole thing worried me. How would my prayers get to him? How would he know what I needed? And then I saw a huge but gentle hand reach into the swirling chaos of wings, and it came out again with just a few butterflies perched on the fingers.

Even at that young age, I knew what God was trying to tell me. My prayers aren't boring little scraps of paper; they are unique, alive and full of colour. That's not because I'm good at prayer; it's because I'm me. The one I pray to doesn't need angels to read and file my prayers. He recognises them instantly, hears them immediately and knows them fully, because he made me. To mix the metaphors a little: when I pray, the notes that reach his ears are unlike any other notes he ever hears. When he created me and you, he designed us so that our voices would be unique, beautiful and instantly recognisable to his ears – not just our physical voices but our prayer voices too.

So how do you find your voice? How do you discover that intimate relationship with God that only you can have? Other people's advice will come in handy, but no one else's prayer life will ever be right for you. The heroes of past centuries may inspire you, the dedication of previous generations may challenge you and the pastor's stories may make you reach higher, but none of them know anything about the prayer life God has in store for you. It's yours to discover and yours to enjoy.

If we're each unique, made by God himself for a never-to-be-repeated communion with him, then it stands to reason that our prayer lives will differ radically. For some of us, the methods of prayer that enliven us most will be the contemplative ones; for others, it will be the activist ones; for some, it will be structures and strategies, whereas for others it will be firing up the intellect. If your prayer 'diet' has been limited, then it's even more likely that you think you're no good at it, because chances are you've never tried the sort of prayer practices that suit your personality – you've not yet learnt to pray the way God made you to pray. Of course, there are disciplines to prayer – we don't always get to do what we enjoy most – but when we begin to access the endless variety and creativity of a one-to-one relationship with the God of the universe, we discover that there is more to prayer than we ever dreamed.

This book takes you on a tour of twelve different types of prayer, introducing you along the way to a whole host of people from the Bible, each of whom used at least one of these prayer practices, and each of whom learnt to find their own unique and precious connection with God. Before you panic that twelve sounds like a daunting amount of prayer types to learn, let me reassure you that you probably do most of them already, without even thinking about it. My hope is that introducing you to each one in a little more detail will help you to recognise it, explore it and see how it fits with all the others. As you work through each chapter, you will probably find that some types of prayer come more naturally to you than others. That is absolutely fine; it's all part of discovering how your personality shapes the way you pray. A full, healthy prayer rhythm should include all twelve types listed in this book, but it's normal for some to come easily and for some to require more discipline. The aim of the book is to help you build a sustainable, life-giving rhythm of prayer, but, like any rhythm, it will start out feeling clunky and like hard work. Take heart, though: as you get to grips with each different type of prayer, you'll soon find that the rhythm turns into a dance. Before long you'll be moving freely between a whole host of different prayer practices without even thinking about it.

This book is designed to be read in any order you like, so if a particular type of prayer catches your attention and you want to know more, feel free to jump straight to that chapter.

Each section of the book ends with some practical suggestions. There's a 'Trying it' exercise, which you can do to get started on that particular type of prayer, and then there are three 'Sustaining it' exercises, which are designed to help you make that aspect of prayer a permanent part of your prayer rhythm. Again, not all of them will suit you, but I hope you will find plenty that do. Some types of prayer will always be a stretch, but as you try out the different exercises, you may just find one or two that fit your personality in such a way that they make that stretch a bit more joyful.

Prayer in the Making is almost entirely about personal prayer. It includes little on group prayer or prayer in church, but it may nonetheless be a useful resource for small groups who want to explore prayer together. There are 'Talking it' discussion questions at the end of each section, and a group prayer activity at the end of each chapter.

As you read this book, I hope and pray that you will be able to build for yourself a rhythm of prayer that is unique and life-giving. I pray that prayer will never again feel like something you fail at, and that you will never again live under the tyranny of needing to be more like someone else. I pray that you will know the astonishing joy of being one who walks and talks with God, and whose conversations with him change the world.

1

Encounter

Prayer is both conversation and encounter with God... We must know the awe of praising his glory, the intimacy of finding his grace, and the struggle of asking his help, all of which can lead us to know the spiritual reality of his presence.

Tim Keller, *Prayer: Experiencing awe and intimacy with God* (Hodder & Stoughton, 2014)

Face-to-face
Hebrews 1:3; Revelation 1:9–20

When I was about 13, I got to pin a geranium to Margaret Thatcher's coat. She was prime minister at the time, and I was one of two blind people chosen to visit 10 Downing Street, at 8.00 one morning, to raise the profile of the Royal National Institute of Blind People on its annual fundraising day. The geranium in question was like the poppies you can buy for Remembrance Sunday: a paper flower with a pin attached to the back.

I had never pinned one on myself before, let alone anyone else, and as I reached up to attach it to the lapel of her coat, I suddenly realised I had no idea how to do it. The fabric was so thick that I quickly gave up on trying to thread the pin through to bring the point out again. I just had to keep poking it in and hope for the best! There were no yelps of pain, so I assume I didn't puncture the formidable lady. She'd been in Moscow the day before for talks with Mikhail Gorbachev, the leader of the Soviet Union, and her plane had only landed four hours earlier, but despite her lack of sleep and busy day ahead, she seemed keen to stop and talk to us. I was too young to understand much about the politics of the day, but I do remember being a little awestruck at meeting someone so important.

Human beings have always prayed. Prayer forms part of every religion on the face of the earth. Surveys show us that, no matter how 'unreligious' a population may seem to be, there will nonetheless be a high percentage of people who pray. Since time immemorial, people have voiced their fears and longings to a being more powerful than themselves, in the hope that he, she or it will be listening.

But that is not what Christian prayer is. Christian prayer is a face-to-face meeting with someone very important indeed. There's a vast repertoire of spiritual practices on offer these days, all suggesting different ways to find peace within yourself and a harmonious connection to the rest of the universe, but that's not what Christian prayer is. Christian prayer is a relationship with the one who created you, who loves you and who wants to be known by you.

The Bible is full of stories of people who set aside time to pray – to do their spiritual exercises or to pour out their anguish – only to find themselves in conversation with God himself. One of those people was the apostle John. He had known Jesus almost all his life. They were the best of friends during Jesus' ministry on earth, and then John had spent decades teaching others to find and cherish that same friendship. In the last years of his life, banished to the prison island of Patmos for his faith in Jesus, John turned to prayer and found himself face-to-face with his friend again (Revelation 1:9–20).

John's Patmos encounter was with Jesus, God in human form – albeit a breathtakingly glorious human form. Christian prayer is not invoking a force or petitioning a capricious deity; it is getting to know someone. Our creator knew that we would only truly be able to relate to him if he came to us in a form we would recognise, and so he came to us as Jesus, God made man. Christian prayer is about getting to know Jesus, and so discovering the heights and depths of God himself. As the writer to the Hebrews put it:

> The Son is the dazzling radiance of God's splendour, the exact expression of God's true nature – his mirror image!
> HEBREWS 1:3 (TPT)

Of course, if you've done any praying in your Christian life, you'll know that it doesn't tend to result in visions of the risen, glorified Christ every time – though you should never rule out the possibility of that happening. In these post-Pentecost days, Jesus is present with us by his Spirit. In fact, Luke and Paul both call the Holy Spirit 'the Spirit of Jesus' (Acts 16:7; Philippians 1:19). In prayer, we interact with the Spirit of Jesus, even if we don't see him standing in front of us.

John's vision of Jesus is rich in symbolism, and if we can interpret some of those symbols, we get a very good idea of what Christian prayer is meant to be like.

The vision began because Jesus spoke to John (Revelation 1:10). That simple truth is at the heart of prayer. If you have any desire at all to communicate with Jesus, it is because he has first spoken to you, whether you realise it or not. When we pray, we don't make an application to God in the hopes that he'll deign to spare us a little of his time and attention. We hear the whisper of his Spirit drawing us in. He's the one inviting us; all we're doing is responding to his invitation to an encounter. He loves you more than you will ever love him; he cherishes your company more than you will ever cherish his. Prayer comes alive when you come to it knowing that the one who calls you is already there, longing to welcome you in.

If John's description of Jesus tells us anything, it's that he is indescribable. John was trying to find words for beauty and glory personified. The verses in Revelation don't tell us how long he spent in Jesus' presence that day, but I suspect he was lost in wonder for a very long time before he could record any words at all. When the closest description you can find for someone's face is that it is 'like the sun shining in all its brilliance' (Revelation 1:16), then you know you are in the presence of supreme greatness. Christian prayer is not just bringing our needs and concerns to God; it is worship. It is stopping to gaze on the beauty of Christ. It is stepping aside from the world to give honour and praise to the one who holds all things together.

One of the first details John noticed about Jesus was his long robe and golden sash (Revelation 1:13). In scripture, gold tends to denote royalty and authority, and the sash was stretched across Jesus' breast. Did it make John think back to that night – that dark, painful night – when Jesus had eaten with them, just before his crucifixion, and when he, John, had leaned on that very same breast (see John 13:25)? Christian prayer is a perplexing yet exhilarating contradiction: we bow in awe of our great high king, yet we are drawn near to rest in his arms; we stand in reverent honour before royalty, because he is absolute goodness and purity, yet we are invited to lean in close enough to hear his heartbeat.

His gaze moving further up, John next noticed Jesus' hair, which was pure white (Revelation 1:14). In many cultures, white hair signifies wisdom: judges don wigs of white hair to symbolise the wisdom of their office, for instance. For Christians, prayer is where we expect to find understanding and revelation. It is a place of worship and rest, but it is also where we talk through our problems and receive wisdom from our 'Wonderful Counsellor' (Isaiah 9:6).

And then, all of a sudden, John met his Saviour's gaze. Jesus has eyes of blazing fire (Revelation 1:14). Those are the eyes that see you, no matter where you are, no matter what's going on in your life. When it's Jesus you're in relationship with, prayer is all about knowing you're not alone and you're never overlooked. He watches over you, and he sees everything. That may be simultaneously the most comforting and the most sobering news. Christian prayer will bring your life into the clarity of God's gaze. If you'd rather not face the truth about yourself, then don't risk an encounter with Jesus. To be face-to-face with him is to be face-to-face with yourself. But it will also bring you the joy of knowing that he never loses sight of you. No matter how dark things may get, you'll always walk in the glow of those warm, fire-bright eyes.

I often wonder whether John found that fiery gaze a bit too intense at first, since the next thing he did was to look down at Jesus' feet – feet that were 'like bronze glowing in a furnace' (Revelation 1:15). Those feet had been tested in the furnace of obedience, walking the dusty roads of humanity, going wherever the Father sent them. Those were the feet of faithful obedience, and ours are the feet that get to walk in his footsteps. Christian prayer always has an exit sign: we step out of life, we go in to encounter the living God and then he sends us back out into the world. If you never want to be given a job to do, a mountain to climb or a person to care for, then avoid Christian prayer at all costs. If you spend any time at all with the one who lived and loved in this world, then he will send you out to do likewise.

Then, finally, there was the voice: that swirling tumult of tones and cadences (Revelation 1:15). Listening to that voice is the artwork of a lifetime. In Hollywood films, God is usually accorded one deep, sonorous voice with which to speak, but nothing could be further from the descriptions we find in the Bible. His voice is complex and multilayered, yet there is a sharpness to his words – the sharpness of a double-edged sword (Revelation 1:16). Christian prayer is the place where we learn to understand the intricacies of that voice and where we open our lives to the power of those words.

Christian prayer is always an encounter. Whether it's a five-second 'arrow prayer' to God at a difficult moment or a couple of hours in his glorious company, it is never just a religious duty or a psychological sticking plaster. It is a face-to-face, heart-to-heart, Spirit-to-spirit connection with him who is the first and the last, the beginning and the end, the king of kings, and the lover of your soul.

Trying it

If Christian prayer starts with Jesus, then it can help to spend some time looking at a picture of him. If you enjoy using your imagination, you might want to picture him in your mind. What do you imagine he looked like while he was here on earth? Or perhaps you'd rather imagine what he looks like now, seated at the right hand of God the Father. Alternatively, you could look for some famous artworks that depict Jesus. You could do an internet search and look through a few images until you come across one that you like or find interesting.

However you find your picture of Jesus, spend some time looking at him. What would it be like to be in his company? What do you want to say to him? What do you think he wants to say to you?

Talking it

- Who's the most famous person you've ever met?
- When did you first learn about Jesus? What do you remember liking most about him, when you first heard about him?
- Christian prayer is meant to be multifaceted. Looking at the pointers from John's vision, is there a facet of prayer you'd like to experience more of?

Sustaining it

1 Become aware
Before you start praying, take a moment to become aware of yourself and what's around you. Sometimes we think we need to shut ourselves off from everything, in order to become aware of God's presence, but the Spirit of Jesus is more solid and more present than anything else in this world. He is more real than the air you're breathing, the chair you're sitting on or this book in your hands, so don't switch your senses off. Open your eyes, breathe deeply, let all your senses come alive and ask him to help you sense his presence.

2 Speak out loud

If you're someone who dreads the thought of praying out loud, don't shut the book just yet. Praying out loud when you're with others can indeed be daunting, but for now I'm just suggesting you speak out loud to God when you're alone. It may only be a few words, but it will help you to connect with the truth that you're communicating with someone else who is real and alive, rather than just talking to yourself in your own head.

3 Make a mini prayer station

When you're developing the habit of encountering the invisible Spirit of Jesus, it can be helpful to have things around you which you can see and touch, to help you focus on him. If you have a place where you usually pray – a favourite chair, for instance – you could put a table next to it with a few objects that are meaningful to you, and that make you think of Jesus. Better still, make up a prayer box that can go with you wherever you pray.

Heart-to-heart
Matthew 6:5–8; Luke 18:9–17

If you were an ancient Roman, prayer was a complicated business. Firstly, you had to have a shrine somewhere in your home, preferably with a fire that burned 24 hours a day, and that's where you'd keep the statues of your favourite gods. You'd be expected to make time to pray at your shrine at least once a day, but it wasn't a straightforward business. You'd have to make sure you were clean and tidy, because dirt and unsavoury smells counted as bad omens, and they could cancel out any praying you did. You'd have to prepare your offering, to convince the gods of your sincerity, and then you'd have to make sure you knew exactly what you were going to pray. In fact, if you didn't have a friendly priest on hand to lead you through some top-of-the-range prayers, you'd probably choose to write a prayer out, to make sure it said exactly what you wanted it to say. The Roman gods were famous for being picky when it came to prayers; they would take offence if you got their names wrong, or if you asked them for too much without flattering them enough first. They were highly legalistic, so Roman prayers read more like legal contracts, because the gods would use any loophole they could to get out of answering your requests. And if all of that wasn't complicated enough, you had to be able to say your prayers without slipping up once. If you got a single word wrong, then you'd have to make a *piaculum* – a little sacrifice to apologise for messing up – and then you'd have to start the whole session over again.

Jesus, God made man, stepped right into the middle of that Roman empire, with all its convoluted religion, and spoke these few ground-breaking sentences:

> But when you pray, go into your room, close the door and pray to your Father, who is unseen. Then your Father, who sees what is done in secret, will reward you. And when you pray, do not keep on babbling like pagans, for they think they will be heard because of their many words. Do not be like them, for your Father knows what you need before you ask him.
> MATTHEW 6:6–8

Most of his listeners would have been Jews, but they would have known about Roman prayer, and these words would have had a special resonance for them as they watched Roman culture seeping ever further into their lives. Jesus was turning everything on its head. In the empire of Rome, prayer was a matter of scrupulous preparation, trying to get it right with your lengthy, perfectly formed compositions and still having no guarantee whatsoever that you'd been heard. In the kingdom of God, prayer would be a simple matter of stepping aside to be in the company of the Father, expressing yourself in uncomplicated sincerity and knowing beyond all doubt that you'd been heard. Prayer wasn't to be difficult, complicated and inaccessible; it was to be as simple as sitting down to talk with a loved one.

John's vision on Patmos reminds us that we come to one who is holy, exalted and glorious, and we should never lose sight of that, but Jesus' words here in the sermon on the mount remind us that our great and mighty God doesn't want us to put up a front to impress him. He knows and loves us just as we are, and he means prayer to start in the most unpretentious corners of our hearts.

Trying to impress the divine wasn't just a Roman trait. Jesus' own people had their fair share of religious nonsense. During one of his other teaching sessions, he told the story of two men who prayed (Luke 18:9–14). The first was a religious man who knew all the right forms and rituals and who was pretty convinced of his own prowess when it came to prayer. The other man was a tax collector – which, in Jesus' time, was code for 'nasty bloke' – and he prayed a rather clumsy, broken prayer from the depths of his soul. The religious man's prayer was all about proving himself to God. The tax collector's prayer was all about bringing his flaws and failings to God and asking for mercy.

There is no such thing as being too bad for God. No matter who you are, what you're like or what you've done, that 'inner room' of prayer is open to you. It's not a literal inner room (though it is a good idea to find a quiet place when you want to have an honest, in-depth conversation with God); it is the inner room of yourself – the place where the real you lives, where all the pretences are stripped away and where you hide the tenderest parts of yourself. That is the place where the one who loves you wants to meet with you in prayer.

In Luke's gospel, this story is followed by another one with the same message. There were parents who wanted their children to see Jesus, but the disciples decided that this wasn't an important enough use of his time, so they sent them away (Luke 18:15–17). Yet Jesus didn't see these little ones as any less welcome or less worthy of his time than anyone else. These were the very ones he felt at home with, because these were the ones who reminded him of home.

Christian prayer means starting small. If you ever feel you're not sophisticated enough, theological enough, articulate enough or holy enough to pray, then you are in exactly the right frame of mind for an encounter with God. He loves simplicity, honesty and humility; those are the hallmarks of his kingdom, and when he finds them in you, he feels completely at home.

Trying it

Find a photo of yourself and spend some time looking at it. As you do so, talk to God about what you see. What do you like about yourself? What do you dislike? What are you proud of? What would you like to change? As you reflect, remember that the Spirit of Jesus is in you and all around you. You are loved wholly and completely by the God who welcomes you – every part of you – into his embrace.

Talking it

- This book is about Christian prayer, but have you ever tried any other kinds of prayer? What was the experience like?
- Have you ever had a time when you didn't feel you could approach God in prayer? What made you feel that way?
- What does it mean to become more childlike in prayer?

Sustaining it

1 Practise the Examen
The Examen is a spiritual exercise from the Ignatian monastic tradition, and it helps you to look back over your day in an honest, prayerful way. Take some time to ask yourself these four questions:

1 What have been the memorable moments of today?
2 What one thing am I most thankful for about today?
3 What have I done today that I need to ask forgiveness for, either of God or of others?

4 When I think about tomorrow, what am I looking forward to and what am I anxious about?

2 Practise brutal honesty

You may not wish to stand on the street and beat your chest like the tax collector in Jesus' story, but brutal honesty is a good discipline to develop. Make it a habit to invite the light of God's grace to shine into the darkest corners of yourself, telling him the things you never tell anyone else, asking his forgiveness for the things you're ashamed of and inviting him to show you the things he wants to set you free from.

3 Practise childlike prayer

Prayers written by or for children can be a truly refreshing addition to your prayer rhythm. They cut through the layers of grown-up complexity, and they bring you back again and again to the simple things of life. Why not buy a children's prayer book or search out some children's prayer resources online? If you have children yourself, you could spend some time writing prayers together. Working with them will help you to keep your own prayers simple.

Group prayer activity

Print off a range of pictures of Jesus, ensuring there's at least one for each person in the group. Lay them on the floor in the middle of the room and invite people to choose one they like or find interesting. Then invite each person to share why they chose their picture. Close with a time of prayer, inviting people to speak out the characteristics of Jesus they love most.

- - - - - - - - -

2

- - - - - - - -

Worship

Like supernatural effervescence, praise will sometimes bubble up from the joy of simply knowing Christ. Praise like that is… delight. Pure pleasure! But praise can also be supernatural determination. A decisive action. Praise like that is… quiet resolve. Fixed devotion. Strength of spirit.

Joni Eareckson Tada, *Glorious Intruder: God's presence in life's chaos* (Multnomah, 1989)

Presence and praise
Psalm 18; 104

I remember so clearly the time I was first surprised by the presence of God. Some friends and I were midway through a Romany caravan holiday in southern Ireland, and we had left our beautiful little wagon and Romeo, our unflappable pony, in a field so we could visit a local beauty spot. Glendalough is an ancient monastic settlement that was founded by St Kevin in the sixth century. It sits in a valley at the confluence of two rivers, and ruins of the original stone buildings can still be seen there today. The rivers have created two lakes in the valley, and there is a particular place where you can watch the river Poulanass thundering into the upper lake. That's where I was standing when it happened.

I was brought up in a Christian family. I've attended church all my life. I have been a follower of Jesus for as long as I have had even the simplest understanding of what that meant. Throughout my teenage years, I had the privilege of attending some amazing Christian events, and I would regularly sense the presence of God in times of sung worship and corporate prayer, but it was in that valley on a sunny afternoon, buffeted by the wind and almost deafened by the roar of the water, that I had the most overwhelming experience of God's presence that I had ever known. It wasn't just that the beauty made me think of him; it was that nature itself seemed to be shouting his presence to me.

As I look back at that time, the thing that strikes me most is how badly I longed to respond to that shout. I was a rather insecure 18-year-old, and I was extremely aware of my two friends nearby, so I just stood still and tried to contain the surge of emotion, but had they not been there – had I been sure I was alone – I think I would have greeted the water's roar with a roar of my own – something wild and jubilant. And you know what? I think that would have been the first time I'd ever really praised from the depths of myself. As it was, even the tidal wave of emotion that I battled to contain felt like no kind of worship I'd ever known. I'd spent years singing songs to God, pouring out my love and devotion in the best way I knew how, but I had never before wanted to yell for sheer joy at his goodness. I knew praise was important: I had long been practising the art of telling him all the things I liked most about him, but that encounter with him at Glendalough had me bursting with something altogether more exuberant. As we discovered in the last chapter, when you encounter the living God, the first thing that happens in you is worship.

King David was a man who encountered God regularly. If you read the stories of his life, you'll get to know a man for whom God was no theoretical ideology, no pagan totem. God's presence was lived experience for him. In his youth, he was engaged to play the harp for King Saul, because when he played, God's presence drove away the darkness in Saul's soul (1 Samuel 16:14–23). Having tasted encounter with God at such a young age, it was something he pursued throughout his life, and it is no coincidence that he is one of the people in the Bible whom we most associate with praise and worship. As he encountered God, praise welled up in him. As praise welled up, he tasted more and more of God's exhilarating company.

Praise isn't a set of theories or philosophies about God. It is always the result of experience. Whether it's an experience of God's presence or an experience of one of those many good gifts, praise always comes from what we know of God. The more we experience of him, the more we praise. If you read David's words of praise (they make up almost half the book of Psalms), you'll see that they always spring from experience, never from theory. That's why it helps to actively put yourself in places where you are likely to experience God.

It was while David was walking the landscape and encountering God in the beauty of creation that some of his most poetic praise bubbled up. Psalm 104 is a case in point.

> Mountains pushed up, valleys spread out in the places you assigned them. You set boundaries between earth and sea; never again will earth be flooded. You started the springs and rivers, sent them flowing among the hills. All the wild animals now drink their fill, wild donkeys quench their thirst.
> PSALM 104:8–11 (MSG)

Nature was something of a 'thin place' for David. 'Thin places' are what Christian communities down the centuries have called areas where the veil between heaven and earth seems thin, where God's presence seems more tangible. When David contemplated creation, he tasted the presence of the creator, and praise flowed.

Do you have a thin place? Glendalough was a thin place for me, and I have found many others since. Your thin place is the location where you sense God's presence in a deeper, more intense way than anywhere else. There's no rhyme or reason to where it is; you might find that it is outside, among nature, or in an ancient church, or a spot with a spectacular view over a city, or even the chair beside your child's bed while they're sleeping. If you want to develop the art of praise, then finding your thin place is a good place to start. As you sense God's presence, you will find that praise surges up within you quite naturally. At first, it will be praise for what you're seeing – you'll notice the beauty of something you're looking at, or you'll catch your breath at the grandeur of your surroundings or the intricacy of something tiny and fragile. But don't let it stop there. Ask yourself what that beauty tells you about the one who created it.

David had another kind of thin place – his memory. If he wasn't worshipping God amid glorious scenery, in the splendour of the tabernacle or in the exuberance of a public procession, then he was meeting him in the sanctuary of his memory, where he stored the treasures of all that God had done for him. In Psalm 18, David's praise bubbled up not from a reaction to the outside world, but from a memory of a deeply personal inner experience. He was remembering a time when God had rescued him from a dark place, and the praise that sprang from that memory forms the basis for one of the most famous psalms of all.

> But me he caught – reached all the way from sky to sea; he pulled me out of that ocean of hate, that enemy chaos, the void in which I was drowning. They hit me when I was down, but God stuck by me. He stood me up on a wide-open field; I stood there saved – surprised to be loved!
>
> PSALM 18:16–19 (MSG)

How often do you visit the storehouse of your memory to look back over the things God has done for you? That's one of the best places to go when you want to stir deep, heartfelt praise. It's also handy because you can do it anywhere, even when your physical surroundings are less than inspiring. Notice how David made his memories into stories, reliving the experience, not just to tell the events, but also to sing the praises of the one who walked through those events with him. Your memory is probably a mixed bag, and there may be things in there you'd rather not relive, but there will be much in that bag that tells of God's goodness, and revisiting it in a prayerful way can lead to a powerful encounter with him. Perhaps, like David, you can remember times when it felt as though God was absent, but looking back, you realise that he was present with you all along, upholding you through dark times. Remembering those moments can be a beautiful way to start praising.

Trying it

Make time to visit a thin place this week. Go to a place where you often feel closer to God, or where his presence somehow seems more tangible. Spend time there, enjoying your surroundings and noticing the handiwork of God in the things you can see and hear. As you do so, notice the feelings, thoughts and words about God that bubble up in you. This is your praise, and it is precious to God. If you're able to do so, why not speak some of it aloud to him?

Talking it

- Do you have a thin place? If so, where is it, and why do you think it is special to you?
- Is there a particular life experience that, when you look back at it, always causes praise to well up in you?
- Have you ever come across anything in art, music or literature that has struck you as a real shout of praise to God?

Sustaining it

1 Awakened by wonder

One of the best ways to stir your soul to praise is to glimpse the wonders of creation. If you're fortunate enough to have some magnificent scenery to hand, take time to drink it in on a regular basis. If not, the internet provides countless opportunities to marvel at creation. You could explore the wonders of the cosmos, read about the intricacies of DNA or just spend a while smiling at the strange things animals do.

2 Record your praise

You may not consider yourself to be as good a poet as David was, but there are plenty of ways to record your praise. When you're visiting your thin place, for instance, you could take a notebook and write down the praise thoughts that bubble up in you. If words aren't your thing, you could take photos and keep them as a 'praise log'. Or you could collect something and take it home as a reminder of the goodness of God: a stone from the beach or a leaf from a tree in the woods, perhaps.

3 Share it

Praise multiplies when we tell someone else. This is particularly true when it comes to revisiting the storehouse of memory. When David wrote Psalm 18, he wasn't just telling his story to himself – he was telling it to others, too. If you have been inspired again by reliving an experience of God from the past, why not share the story with someone else?

Grief and gratitude
Psalm 51:17; Luke 7:36–50

In stark contrast to my experience at Glendalough, I remember a season during my university years when worship was an altogether less exuberant business. I was in the kitchen at my dad's house – a significantly less picturesque location, with no thundering rivers and no ineffable sense of God's presence. Disappointment after disappointment had piled up on me, and I felt as though I was losing the plot. Worshipping God was just about the last thing I felt like doing, but I had been taught well, so I knew this was precisely the time to press in and praise him anyway.

My song of choice was one we sang often in our student group at university, but as I opened my mouth to sing, a wave of weeping hit me. Nothing daunted, I croaked out the first line of the song between gulping sobs, 'You make my heart feel glad!' As the words left my lips, the irony of the situation wasn't lost on me. I laughed out loud. I could almost hear God saying, 'You could've fooled me!'

Worship can be the jubilant overflow of a joyful heart, but it can also be a gift given at great cost in turbulent times. Luke's gospel tells the story of a woman who knew the true price of worship (Luke 7:36–50). So desperate was her longing for an encounter with Jesus, so urgent her desire to pay him homage, that she plucked up the courage to interrupt dinner at the house of Simon the Pharisee, an important religious leader. In the thick of judgement and disapproval, she brought Jesus three offerings, each of which has something to teach us about worship.

Luke tells us that she led 'a sinful life' (Luke 7:37). Some speculate that she was a prostitute, and some wonder if she was Mary Magdalene. We don't know for sure on either count, but we do know that she came to Jesus with a weight of guilt on her soul. She was known in the local town as a woman of ill repute, and the guests at the dinner table probably thought their suspicions were confirmed when she started kissing Jesus' feet, weeping on them and then wiping them with her hair (Luke 7:38). It would have been seen as an act of gross indecency for a woman to take down her hair in public in those days, but that didn't stop her. Perhaps she thought she was already so bad that nothing could sink her any lower in Jesus' estimation. Some of us might have tried to cover up a bit – to make ourselves look as acceptable as we could, until we were sure Jesus would forgive us – but not this woman. She didn't try to finesse her sin away. She came to Jesus, raw and honest, bringing her contrition as her worship.

In our success-conscious world, it is easy to assume that Jesus wouldn't want to be worshipped by someone whose life had veered off into sin. Won't he reject our offering if we're 'damaged goods'? That seems to be what Simon thought should happen, but mercifully it's not Jesus' way. Worship starts when we bring ourselves, sin and all, to his feet. To acknowledge our shame and to ask for his forgiveness and healing – that is as powerful a poem of worship as any of David's nature psalms.

Along with her contrition, the woman brought her grief. She wept. She wept for her sin and shame, but she must also have wept for the pain, sorrow and rejection she would have experienced in a society that had written her off. If you have ever grieved, you will know that it doesn't feel terribly worshipful. It feels messy and futile, and though we may draw comfort from the fact that God loves and welcomes us, it hardly feels as though we are bringing him any kind of worship worthy of the name. So Jesus' response is remarkable. He likens her tears to the ceremonial washing that would have been offered to an honoured guest – that should have been offered to him, but that Simon hadn't bothered to do (Luke 7:44). I suspect the guests were aghast at the idea that this sinful woman's tears were as pure to Jesus as the cleansing water in Simon's wash-jars.

When you bring your grief to God, you are not bothering him; you are honouring him. When you pour out the pain in your heart, it isn't self-indulgence; it's worship. Earlier in this chapter we talked about 'thin places'. Some of the thinnest places I've ever known have been the places where I've grieved. Indeed, that kitchen in my dad's house became a thin place, as I realised that God didn't need me to muster up a glad heart. He didn't need my praise to be joyful before he could accept it. He simply received my sorrow as an offering of worship.

Lastly, the woman brought Jesus the most precious thing she owned. She brought him the jar of perfume that would have cost a year's wages, which, before the invention of bank accounts, probably constituted her life savings. And having brought it, she broke it and poured it out on him, so that she would never be able to get it back. And with that one action, she 'threw away' the most valuable thing she had, making her already tough life even tougher.

If life has proved costly for you, then take heart from this woman's story. Each time we give something up for the sake of the God we love, each time we lose what we can't get back, it is counted as worship by the one who knows better than anyone what it cost us. Again, Jesus used the woman's action to draw attention to Simon's shortcomings, comparing her perfume to the anointing oils that Simon might have considered offering a special guest in his home (Luke 7:46). Given that a bottle of perfume like hers would often have been used by a prostitute to drum up trade, and that is almost certainly what the assembled company thought hers was for, it would have been shocking to hear Jesus likening it to the oil used to pamper the guests of wealthy households. But this was grace personified. He knew that by bringing her most precious possession, she was worshipping him, and that to him was an honour greater than any other. No amount of VIP treatment would have blessed him as much as that sacrificial gift.

Does it ever occur to you that your worship brings God joy? We tend to think of worship as something we owe God, so we assume he receives it in much the same way the credit card company receives our money when we pay off the debt. But that's not how Jesus received this woman's worship. He didn't pat her on the head, whisper a hasty 'Well done, dear' and send her packing before she could embarrass them all any further. No, he stopped what he was doing, turned his full attention to her and received each of her offerings with reverent respect. Of course, God is worthy of our worship, but he also enjoys it because he enjoys us.

We'll finish this chapter with some words from another of David's most famous prayers, because though they were written centuries earlier, they seem to capture the beauty of this woman and her worship.

> My sacrifice, O God, is a broken spirit; a broken and contrite
> heart you, God, will not despise.
> PSALM 51:17

Whether you are bubbling over with exuberant praise or falling at his feet with nothing to offer but a broken heart and a contrite spirit, know that he welcomes you just the same, and that your worship touches his heart.

Trying it

When we come to God in prayer, it's tempting to try to edit ourselves – to steer clear of things in our lives that we think he may disapprove of, or to gloss over things that have caused us significant pain, for fear that the emotion will overwhelm us. At some point in the next few days, spend half an hour or so sitting with him. Take with you into that prayer time an object that signifies an area of shame or pain in your life. It may be something that reminds you of a sin or failure, or it may be something you associate with a season of grief. The aim is not to think about the object or pray about the issue it represents. The aim is simply to sit and hold it in God's presence, as a symbol of the fact that you are bringing your whole self to him in worship.

Talking it

- Can you imagine a 21st-century version of the story in Luke 7:36–50? What would be our modern-day equivalent of someone braving the scorn and judgement of others to bring costly worship to Jesus?
- Have you been through a season of grief? What did it teach you about God and about worship?
- Have you ever given up something extremely precious as worship to God?

Sustaining it

1 Worship with full confession
Guilt and shame will kill your prayer life faster than almost anything. Full confession means bringing to Jesus your guilt for the things you've done wrong, but it also means bringing your shame – that

crushing feeling of being judged by others. He wants to forgive you and set you free. By meeting Jesus right in front of her accusers, the woman in Luke 7 not only repented of her sin, but she also confronted her own sense of shame. She was forgiven, of course, but her shame was also exchanged for honour. That's why we're still talking about her today.

2 Worship with grief

It is easy to assume that God won't want to keep hearing the same old prayers about the same old aches and pains. If something has hurt you or you're grieving, make a habit of bringing that wound to God. It's not a self-centred rant; it's an offering of worship, and he will meet you in it.

3 Break a pot

A broken pot can be a powerful symbol of what it means to worship God with our whole selves. Acquire a pot that you don't need for anything else. You probably don't have alabaster, but choose one made of pottery rather than glass or plastic. Put it into a strong carrier bag, then take it outside and break it using something heavy, such as a hammer. Extricate the pieces carefully, then take them into your next prayer time. As you look at them and hold them, reflect on what it means to give your broken pieces to Jesus in worship.

Group prayer activity

Testimony is a beautiful way to worship together. Invite each member of the group to share a short story about something they're thankful to God for.

3

Listening

To pray is to listen to the One who calls you 'my beloved daughter', 'my beloved son', 'my beloved child'. To pray is to let that voice speak to the centre of your being, to your guts, and let that voice resound in your whole being.

Henri Nouwen, 'Moving from solitude to community to ministry', *Leadership Journal* (Spring 1995)

Recognising God's voice
1 Samuel 3:1–10; 16:1–13

Do you have an 'It's me' person? 'It's me' people are those who, when they phone, you know exactly who they are just from hearing them say those two little words. 'It's me' people are the ones whose voices you'd know anywhere.

Is God an 'It's me' voice in your life? Most of us know at least one person whose voice we would instantly recognise, and yet many of us would say we don't find it easy to hear and recognise the voice of the God we love and serve. In fact, we often feel that we fail when it comes to listening to him and discerning what he's saying.

The good news, at the start of this adventure, is that the God who walks with us does not want to be a silent companion. He fully intends you to hear him clearly and to recognise him as easily as you recognise your nearest and dearest. One of the most joyous truths about prayer is that it's the place where we learn to recognise his voice and to hear his wisdom.

Before the arrival of the Holy Spirit at Pentecost, most of God's people had no expectation of having a 'personal' relationship with God. Only a few of the most holy men and women had the privilege of walking and talking with him on a daily basis, and one of those people was a prophet called Samuel.

Samuel needed to be able to recognise God's voice. He went on to become a wise and renowned prophet in Israel, a man much trusted for his ability to hear from God, but in the story in 1 Samuel 3:1–10, he was still a boy, having his beginner's lesson in distinguishing God's voice from the other voices in his life. It's no coincidence that he was in the temple, sleeping by the altar, resting in the very presence of God. We need to be able to hear God anywhere, at any time, but the place of prayer is the best place to begin the lesson.

It's easy to assume that the prophets could all hear God with perfect clarity from day one, but when Samuel first heard God's voice, he didn't know whose it was (1 Samuel 3:4–5). Thanks to the outpouring of God's Spirit at Pentecost, it is now our privilege to walk and talk with God every day of our lives, if we want to. Yet we forget that it takes time to learn the art of it. We tend to set the bar very high for ourselves, thinking that we should immediately be able to hear him speaking long, complex messages to us, but, like Samuel, we need to start with the basics.

The first thing Samuel learnt was how to recognise when God was trying to get his attention. The story gives the impression that he heard an audible voice calling him, and this can immediately make us feel inadequate; we've never heard that voice, so we must be doing something wrong. In truth, relatively few people say they hear God's voice audibly, but that's not because we're all failing. It's because God simply isn't restricted to words and soundwaves. He has every dimension of reality available to him, and he can 'speak' to you in a thousand different ways. He can whisper a thought into your mind, sing into your heart or write in letters of fire in the sky above your head. Just because you don't hear him like you hear your human friends, don't be fooled into thinking you're deaf or he's ignoring you.

The adventure for each one of us is to learn to notice when God is getting our attention. It takes practice, and you'll need the Spirit's help, but there is nothing more exhilarating than knowing that the God of the universe is speaking to you. Perhaps it will be a nudge in your thoughts or a sight that catches your eye. Perhaps it will be a sudden sense of his presence or a phrase you hear someone say. Whatever it is, it will be something that suddenly turns your thoughts towards him. Once you hear it, don't write it off as 'just one of those things'. It is highly likely to be God calling to you, so, wherever you are and whatever you're doing, take a moment to answer him, 'Here I am, Lord. I'm listening.' Then stay alert for what he might want to show you or say to you. In these early days of your Samuel lesson, you'll probably find God doesn't immediately download a world-changing message to your brain. In fact, it may seem like he's got nothing to say at all. That's okay; this is practice at noticing and recognising his voice. Just enjoy the pleasure of connecting with him in that moment.

Relationship always starts with a name. If you want to get to know someone or to communicate something important to them, one of the first things you do is find out what they're called. When you want to start a conversation with someone, the polite way to get their attention is to use their name. From Samuel's response, we can assume that the very first thing he heard God say was 'Samuel' (1 Samuel 3:4).

Have you ever heard God speak your name? I don't necessarily mean the name your parents gave you; I mean the name he knows you by. In the Bible, when God calls someone's name, he often adds a term of affection: for instance, Mary was 'highly favoured' (Luke 1:28),

Daniel was 'highly esteemed' (Daniel 10:11) and Gideon was 'mighty warrior' (Judges 6:12). Why not ask God to tell you the name he calls you by? It may be connected to your actual name or something completely different. It may be a word or phrase he draws your attention to in scripture or a character trait that others often affirm in you. Just remember, God speaks in many different ways, so keep your mind, heart, ears and eyes open, and let him tell you in his own time. Whatever his name for you is, it will be something meaningful and loving.

There's nothing magical or mystical about this, and there are no right answers. It's simply about practising hearing God's words of affirmation over you. He may use different names during different seasons of your life, but the name will always reflect the deep affection he has for you, and as such it will be a precious gift every time you hear it. When you've got an idea of what name he wants to call you by, remember to look and listen out for it as you go about your daily life.

Later in his life, Samuel had another experience that gives us insight into how to recognise God's voice (1 Samuel 16:1–13). Many years had passed, and God had instructed him to anoint Israel's second king. Samuel knew which family the king would come from, but had no idea which son it would be. As Jesse, head of the family, paraded his beloved sons before the prophet, we get a glimpse of Samuel's very simple discernment process – a kind of 'thumbs up, thumbs down' conversation with God (1 Samuel 16:7–11). For each son that came to him, Samuel sensed the 'No' from God. Only when David came in did Samuel sense God's resounding 'Yes'.

How familiar are you with God's thumbs-up, thumbs-down response? When we learn a foreign language, the first words we usually pick up are 'Yes' and 'No'. We start there because these are among the simplest concepts to communicate. The same principle is true in our communications with God. Long before we learn to hear complex messages from him, we need to get familiar with his negative and his affirmative. As you make choices, listen out for the opinion of heaven. You're no robot, so God won't communicate an opinion on every decision you make, but listen out for those moments when he does. Don't worry about trying to understand his reasons at this stage; just practise noting and obeying his 'Yes' and his 'No'.

In all the listening you do, remember that the God you listen to is the God who loves you. Whether he's saying 'Yes' or 'No', or just calling your name to get your attention, he is speaking to you in love. If the voice you hear sounds accusing or oppressive, simply take it to God in prayer and ask him to tune your ears to the frequencies of his love.

Trying it

Other people are often better at affirming us than we are at affirming ourselves, so they may be able to help you hear the name God wants to give you. Ask a few of your friends to give you two or three positive words that they would use to describe you. When all the words are in, write them on a piece of paper and take them to your prayer time. Meditate on them, and ask God to draw your attention to one that he particularly wants you to hear at this time. Of course, as you reflect on the words, they may prove to be just a starting place, and he may give you a different name altogether.

Talking it

- Have you ever known God to get your attention in an unusual or surprising way?
- Have you ever heard God say something to you and been absolutely sure it was him? What did he say and why were you able to recognise his voice so clearly?
- Much damage can be done when people claim to have heard God's voice and use it as a justification to do harmful things. Have you ever been in a situation where you've had to question whether someone has really heard God?

Sustaining it

1 Practise naming others

Just as we benefit when others encourage us, so it benefits others when we encourage them, because it helps them to tune into God's words of loving kindness. Take time to encourage others by telling them what you like most about them. Develop the habit of using affirming words, even in the simplest of communications – for instance, instead of just saying, 'Thanks for doing that,' say, 'Thank you for being so thoughtful in taking time to do that for me.'

2 Practise the art of being stoppable

No matter how busy or preoccupied you become, make a point of stopping whenever something catches your attention.

- Stop when you see or hear something beautiful, shocking or unusual.
- Stop when you read a verse of scripture that 'jumps out' at you.
- Stop when you feel particularly moved by something.
- Stop when you encounter an unexpected event.

As soon as your attention is caught, stop in your tracks (literally, if possible), and invite God to speak to you. Whether or not you hear anything further, the stopping is a moment of worship.

3 Practise sensing the 'yes/no' nudge

Invite God into your dilemmas. When you come across a decision you need to make, choose the option you think best, then stop for a moment and invite God to nudge you – to give you a sense of his 'Yes' or his 'No'. Remember, it may not be a simple right/wrong alternative, so don't be discouraged if you don't sense anything, but making the space for him to speak is an important act of trust and surrender.

Listening with the senses
Zechariah 1:8–21, 4:1–14, 6:9–14

Bad days come to us all – even the rich, famous and successful. Fred Astaire was once told by an MGM casting director that he couldn't sing, couldn't act and could only dance 'a little'. Steve Jobs, creator of such 21st-century icons as the iPod and the iPad, actually got fired from Apple shortly after launching the company. There is colour, humour and beauty in our world that wouldn't be there if those men had taken no for an answer. But they kept looking for ways to share their creativity, and eventually their talents were acknowledged.

One of the most unfortunate trends in Christian history has been to dismiss things like art and creativity as 'secular' pastimes with little to offer in the way of spiritual enrichment. Yet beauty and imagination not only enhance our lives, they also show us God. How often has a painting, a piece of music or a powerful story communicated the truths of God to you in a way that no watertight theological argument ever could? It shouldn't surprise us, really, since the God we serve is the creator of all things. Why would he not want to use the full breadth of his created realm to communicate with us?

Zechariah was a prophet who encountered a truly creative side to God's communication style. He lived at a time when the people of Israel were rebuilding their temple, after a long season in captivity. The renovations had hit some roadblocks, and God commissioned Zechariah and Haggai to speak to the people and their leaders on his behalf to get the work moving again. Haggai seems to have heard God's words and passed them on in a rather conventional way, but nothing was quite that simple for Zechariah. Instead of statements, he got questions; instead of explanations, he got surreal visions; instead of a sermon, he got a 3D multimedia experience. There were some words in the midst of it all, but the messages were threaded through the images and the atmosphere of those visions, as much as through the words that accompanied them.

God had things to tell Israel through Zechariah, and he used the full breadth of the prophet's senses and imagination to communicate with him. In one of the visions, it's as though Zechariah's view shifted between what he was seeing with his physical eyes – the building works for the new temple (Zechariah 4:8–10) – and what he was seeing with the eyes of his imagination – angels and gold lampstands (Zechariah 4:2–3). By the creative Spirit of God, it was all woven together into a tapestry of challenge and encouragement for its intended audience.

Have you developed the habit of listening with your eyes – or, for that matter, your nose, hands or taste buds? Do you expect God to 'speak' in colours, fragrances and symphonies, as much as in words? Having learnt to recognise when God is getting your attention, the next challenge is to fling wide your expectations, so that you can hear him with all your senses and even your imagination.

There is one particular question God asked Zechariah several times during their conversations: 'What do you see?' (Zechariah 4:2). In fact, you will find many of the other prophets in the Bible being asked the same question. It's as though God was challenging them to switch on their senses, to take in the full dimensions of what he was showing them. Suddenly, the prophetic revelation wasn't just a download session where God spoke and the prophet listened; it became a conversation: the prophet looking around, exploring the scene and seeking to understand, while God painted the shapes and shades that would communicate what he wanted to say.

As a blind person, one of the things that fascinates me most is how little sighted people actually see of their surroundings. I am constantly amazed, for instance, at how little awareness the average London commuter has of what's going on around them as they plough their weary furrow to and from work. We humans easily get stuck in the rut of what we know, and one of the reasons we need to learn to listen to God with all of our senses is that it shifts us from oblivious to alert, and we're suddenly able to see things we hadn't noticed before. The more aware we are of our surroundings, the more chance God has of speaking to us through them, and that can be a particularly useful facet of hearing his voice, when life doesn't afford us much time to sit and listen in stillness or silence.

If prayer is, among other things, taking time to listen to God, then it is worth making that 'listening' a multisensory experience. Don't think of the sights and sounds around you as distractions; think of them as things he might use to communicate with you. Whether it's scenery, artwork, music or gourmet cooking, anything that stirs your senses can be a moment of connection with him. Enjoy it, but don't stop at that. Ask him to help you understand what he's saying through it.

You don't have to stick to only the physical senses. Open the eyes of your imagination, just as artists, storytellers and inventors have been doing for centuries, and dream up new possibilities. Zechariah's first recorded vision was a message of hope for Israel (Zechariah 1:8–21). Instead of being a wordy sermon, though, it was a colourful story about horses riding out to test the earth (Zechariah 1:10–11), horns of tyranny being smelted by craftsmen whose art brought freedom and justice (Zechariah 1:18–21) and the angel of the Lord speaking words of kindness and comfort (Zechariah 1:14–17). Stories are so often the places where we hear God's voice most clearly. People who are stuck and overwhelmed, as the Israelites were, need to hear stories of how things can be different, and that's what Zechariah's visions were about.

What stories can you imagine for your loved ones or your local community? What would it look like if God were to answer your prayers for healing, reconciliation or liberation? What would life look like if God's kingdom were more real than the world's way of doing things? As you imagine, ask God to help you see what he wants you to see. As Zechariah shared the fruits of his imagination, led by the Spirit, his visions helped kick-start a whole new season of renewal and regeneration for his people. You never know what your imagination might inspire others to.

We sometimes worry about whether this kind of 'hearing' is really safe. Won't our minds lead us astray? But if you're reading your Bible regularly and spending time in God's presence, then you will learn to distinguish what God's language sounds like. If your senses or your imagination seem to be taking you somewhere that feels foreign to the heart and character of God, then simply invite him to refocus you. Read some scripture, pray for clarity and then look again. Like every kind of communication with God, this takes practice. The more you do it, the more fluent you become.

And one more thing: once you begin to 'hear' God in truly creative ways, don't be surprised if he asks you to use your own creative talents to pass on messages to others. Zechariah got to make a crown for Joshua, the high priest (Zechariah 6:9–14). Perhaps your painting, your home-baked cake or your act of kindness will feature in the multimedia vision that God is showing someone else.

Trying it

Find a story in one of the gospels where Jesus meets someone and changes their life. As you read the story through slowly, imagine you're there, watching events unfold. Put yourself in the shoes of someone who would have been there – a bystander, a disciple or the person whose life Jesus changed.

- What is the physical environment like (the sights, smells, sounds and so on)?
- How does it feel to be so near to Jesus?
- What do you notice about him?
- What would you like to say to him?
- What is it like when his power starts working to change things?

Ask God to speak to you about your own life, as you use your imagination to explore the story.

Talking it

- How do you usually hear God's voice? Having read this chapter, are there other kinds of 'listening' you'd like to explore?
- Has someone else's creativity – a story or a piece of art or music, for instance – ever helped you to hear God's voice? If so, what was it and what did God say to you?
- As churches, how can we encourage more people to share what they're hearing from God, especially when it comes through the creative arts?

Sustaining it

1 Make space for art

Try to form a habit of making space in your life for art: visit a gallery, listen to music or visit a nearby town and admire the architecture. These things are enjoyable, of course, but they're also key moments for opening your senses and allowing God to speak to you.

2 Make time for stories

We learn all about imagination through the stories we hear when we're young – stories of wonderfully impossible things that simply don't exist in the physical world around us. As adults, we still need to cherish stories, because they build our faith and broaden our horizons. Whether you like fiction or accounts of real people, whether you prefer books or films, make time for story.

3 Make room for new experiences

Routine and familiarity can muffle our ears to God's voice, and it is often only when we step into the uncertainty of new experiences that we hear him speaking. Build a habit of trying new things every so often. If one of your friends has a hobby you've never tried, ask if you can join them. If there's a skill you'd like to acquire, look for evening classes or a local club where you could learn it. Challenge yourself with things that stretch you, and come alive to the new things God is saying to you.

Group prayer activity

Listen to God together using your senses. Give each person a drink of water and a sweet to suck. Play a piece of music and invite them to listen while they eat and drink. Afterwards, invite people to share anything they heard from God as they were listening, feeling and tasting.

- - - - - - - - -

4

- - - - - - - - -

Stillness

There's something about sunbathing that tells us more about what prayer is like than any amount of religious jargon. When you're lying on the beach, something is happening, something that has nothing to do with how you feel or how hard you're trying. You're not going to get a better tan by screwing up your eyes and concentrating. You give the time, and that's it. All you have to do is turn up. And then things change, at their own pace. You simply have to be there where the light can get at you.

Rowan Williams, *Pause for Thought*, BBC Radio 2 (October 2005)

Making space to stop
Lamentations 3:19–30; Luke 10:38–42

When I was a child, my mum was the leader of our church Sunday school. Since her day job was being a head teacher, she ran a tight ship, and never more so than when it came to prayer time. I remember the words that always prefaced our moments of prayer, and if you ever went to Sunday school, you might remember them too: 'Sit still, put your hands together and close your eyes.'

I suppose it was a useful method of crowd control, but it was also rooted in an ancient understanding that prayer should, at times, involve a choice to shut out the world around us, so that we can direct all our attention to God. The 'hands together, eyes closed' injunction may be particularly pertinent when it comes to calming a hall full of exuberant children, but praying people have been doing much the same thing for centuries. Monks and nuns have left their labours many times a day to go to the chapel for prayer. Churches have kept their doors open so that people could leave the world outside and seek refuge and strength in the stillness of an ancient place of worship. Many shopping centres now even come equipped with a prayer space, because people the world over understand that the human soul needs space and peace if it is to be truly refreshed.

If stopping to pray has been a habit of believers over the centuries, then we can safely assume it is even more necessary today. A couple of hundred years ago, it would have taken you days to travel any significant distance, and hours to do some of the most basic household chores. The slowness of life helped make space for prayer. Nowadays, I can be on the other side of the world in a day, and I can do several chores at once in my half-hour lunch break, thanks to modern technology. It takes a whole new level of vehement determination to stop and pray these days.

One of Jesus' friends was a woman called Mary, and she had just the kind of vehemence and determination I'm talking about. Luke gives us a glimpse of it in one of the stories in his gospel (Luke 10:38–42). Mary lived in Bethany, probably with her sister Martha and her brother Lazarus, and Jesus frequently used her home as a stopover. The story starts at the moment Jesus arrived on their doorstep. Given the lack of telephone or email communication, we can safely assume that he wouldn't have been able to give them much warning of his arrival, so hospitality would have needed to be a spontaneous business. Perhaps that's why Martha got rather stressed that day, because she didn't have the house ready when he arrived. Yet Mary had no intention of getting stressed or distracted by the practical demands of entertaining. For her, Jesus' arrival was the signal to stop everything else, to shut out the world and to sit at his beloved feet.

Throughout the chapters of this book, we will discover that prayer is multifaceted. It can be done anywhere, pretty much anyhow. God is not stingy about conversation. He loves to be in touch with us, and so he has opened many, many channels of communication. But if all of your prayer is done on the fly, alongside the rest of your busy life, then you are certain to be missing out on something. There is a quality of connection with God that we can only truly find when we make a habit of stepping aside from our everyday lives and choosing to still ourselves in his presence. For some of us, this will come naturally, because our personalities predispose us to loving this kind of prayer. For others, this will be a discipline, because we naturally prefer action and movement. But for all of us, it is absolutely essential to our well-being and to the deepening of our relationship with God.

Jeremiah was a man in deep distress when he wrote the words in Lamentations. He lived at a time of great political turmoil, when his land was being occupied and his people were being enslaved by a foreign power, and he seems to have been rather unpopular – he was even imprisoned in a muddy old cistern once, which is a bit like being thrown down a well. He could have been forgiven for giving up on prayer altogether, but he didn't. In fact, he was at pains to remind people of how important it was to stop and be still before God, particularly when times are tough:

> When life is heavy and hard to take, go off by yourself. Enter the silence. Bow in prayer. Don't ask questions: Wait for hope to appear.
> LAMENTATIONS 3:28–29 (MSG)

If you're anything like me, you may be guilty of reasoning that you can only really afford to stop and sit in God's presence when things are going well: when all the jobs are done, the diary isn't too full, the sun is shining and there's nothing weighing on your mind. Yet these words from Jeremiah are a warning that we can't afford to wait until stillness fits in with our other plans. We must make time to sit quietly and wait, even when life is overwhelming – especially when life is overwhelming. The space and stillness are life-giving to our souls, and the decision to stop is an act of worship in itself. The world may be throwing all sorts of chaos at you, but when you choose to stop, to make space and to still yourself at the feet of Jesus, you make a small but defiant declaration that you trust him, no matter what is going on around you.

I often wonder whether Martha thought Mary would just sit at Jesus' feet for ten minutes or so, as a polite acknowledgement; if so, she couldn't have been more wrong. Mary was in no hurry to move from that place. Did she know the art of real stillness – that our bodies need time to relax, our minds need time to slow and our souls need time to breathe deeply? Somehow, Mary knew that this vital moment of communion with Jesus could not be rushed, skimped on or squeezed into the five minutes between the washing-up and the bed-making.

Whether or not it comes naturally to you, a rhythm of prayer will always need to include the practice of stillness. As you make space to stop, so you settle yourself in a place where the light can get at you.

Trying it

Have you got a few minutes now? Then close the book (once you've read these instructions) and put it down. Settle yourself so you're sitting in an upright position that's as comfortable as possible. You don't need to put your hands together like we did in Sunday school, but you might want to rest your palms on your knees. It's up to you whether you close your eyes or keep them open. Then just stay still for a few minutes. You'll probably find your nose itches, or you hear a strange noise, or you suddenly want to plan a cruise... but don't worry about any of that. Just focus on staying physically still. Notice your breathing slow and your muscles relax, and feel what happens when your world stops spinning, just for a few moments.

That's it – you've started practising stillness.

Talking it

- What's the first thing you would do if Jesus turned up unexpectedly at your house?
- What do you think most gets in the way of you making space to stop and be still?
- If stillness is important in our personal prayer lives, then presumably it's important in the life of the church too. How could we build more 'stillness prayer' into the busyness of church activity?

Sustaining it

1 Find the right time

An unrushed hour or so of stillness may not be something you can fit in every day, but if you examine your week, you may find there is a suitable gap. Ideally it needs to be a time when you know you won't be too sleepy, and when no one will need you for anything, so you can switch your phone off. If you share life with a partner, then why not ask them to help guard that time for you: to look after the children or field your work calls for you? Above all, it needs to be a time that is non-negotiable: decide how long you're going to sit still in God's presence, and don't cut it short for anything less than a major disaster. And if an hour seems impossible to begin with, start with 20 minutes and work your way up. You may soon find that the time flies by quicker than you expect.

2 Find the right place

The sense of place matters more to some people than others. You may be one of those people who can shut yourself away in stillness no matter where you are, or you may be someone who needs the place to feel safe and restful before you can truly settle yourself at Jesus' feet. If you're the latter, then think of a place where you feel safe, or which you find particularly beautiful or inspiring. Wherever you choose to be, make sure it is somewhere you don't feel self-conscious and won't be interrupted or intruded upon. It needs to be a place where you feel free to be yourself. When you're there, find a comfortable position – but not so comfortable that you fall asleep.

3 Use anchors

Mary had the benefit of being able to look at Jesus sitting right there in front of her. You and I have the challenge of tuning ourselves into his Spirit, who we can't see or touch in the same way. Time in stillness can become a baffling maelstrom of thoughts, feelings, cares and fears, and that's okay, but it helps to have anchors – things that keep drawing your attention back to the one in whose presence you are sitting. Reading and speaking have their place in prayer, of course, but they are both activities of the mind, so they prevent us from truly becoming still. Instead, you might like to light a candle and watch the flame, or hold a cross in your hand. You might find it helpful to play music that steers your mind back to God and his goodness. You might like to sit with a picture that inspires you, or a view that stirs your soul. Look for things that draw your thoughts towards God without requiring you to think too hard or move too much – things that help you stay still and centred on Jesus.

Feeling and filling
Lamentations 3:19–30; John 11:20–36

When you practise stillness, you soon learn that your inner world can be a noisy, messy place. I've sometimes reached the end of a time of prayer feeling more exhausted and overwhelmed than I did at the start, because the stillness has simply made space for all my inner turmoil to spill out and drown me. To begin with, I used to think that this meant I'd failed badly in my praying, but over the years I've learnt that it is a natural part of the stillness discipline.

You may remember another story featuring Mary and Martha. John tells of the time when their brother Lazarus became very ill, and Jesus didn't arrive in time to heal him before he died. We know the end of the story, that Jesus raised Lazarus to life again, but we come across Mary and Martha before the miracle has happened and while the grief is still extremely raw (John 11:20–36). It's interesting to notice the difference in their reactions. Martha, for her part, was very 'together', telling Jesus in a matter-of-fact way that she knew he would be able to solve the situation. In contrast, Mary was distraught and angry. Having seen her serenely resting at Jesus' feet (in Luke's gospel), we might logically assume that she would be the one speaking words of faith and hope, but she wasn't.

Stillness in God's presence has the effect of opening up deep places in us. Our western culture has taught us to anaesthetise pain and sorrow by filling our lives with all sorts of comforts and distractions. When we practise stillness, we deliberately push those distractions away, so it stands to reason that the darker thoughts should surface. I wonder whether Mary's grief-stricken outburst was actually a product of her times of stillness with Jesus. To sit with someone in stillness is to make yourself vulnerable to them. To listen to someone is to allow them to speak deeply into your soul. Mary had sat with Jesus and listened to him. Perhaps, then, her grief-stricken outburst wasn't a lack of faith, but the natural reaction of showing her true self to her truest friend.

If stillness makes space for the worst of our thoughts and feelings, it is also where we surrender control. Mary was angry and hurt that Jesus hadn't come sooner. She might reasonably have refused to see him, but she didn't. She knew that she needed to be in his presence, even while she was furious with him. And interestingly, despite the turmoil of her emotions, her posture before him was much the same as it was when he came to her house before. She didn't try to drag him to the tomb or cajole him into doing something. She simply put herself at his feet, honouring him with her worship, even in the midst of her pain (John 11:32). No matter what stirs up in us, when we practise stillness we resolutely refuse to leap up and action our own solutions. We train ourselves to stay still in God's arms, making our simple affirmation that he is in control, and that he will have the last word.

When we practise stillness, we turn our attention away from the hundreds of things in life that offer us a quick fix, and we cast ourselves on the mercy of the one who holds all things together.

I remember a time when my life felt like one great sea of trouble and pain. A dear friend of mine had just died, and I was rapidly coming to the conclusion that I was far from being the person people wanted or needed me to be. I was close to throwing in the towel on a number of things, and every time I settled to prayer, I ended up a soggy mess of snot and tears. One day, I heard the voice of God so clearly that it almost took my breath away. It wasn't an audible voice; it was a voice in my head, but it was unmistakable. The words came accompanied by a picture of a tiny raft in a terrifyingly stormy sea. The raft was floating along, in danger of being smashed up by the waves at any moment, and I was perched precariously on top. The words were brief and to the point: 'Keep still!' For several years afterwards, I would call that image to mind when I felt most distressed. I knew that God was promising to navigate me safely through this awful season, but that I needed to stay still and let him do his work.

Crucial to stillness is not fearing feelings. When everything else has been stripped away – all the noise and busyness that protect us from ourselves – then feelings will surface, whether we like it or not. Jeremiah made no attempt to anaesthetise himself against the pain he was feeling; he just sat with it, and that makes his words pretty hard to read sometimes (Lamentations 3:19–30). Yet surprisingly, this passage contains one of the most hope-filled verses in all of the scriptures:

> Yet this I call to mind and therefore I have hope: Because of the Lord's great love we are not consumed, for his compassions never fail. They are new every morning; great is your faithfulness.
> LAMENTATIONS 3:21–23

If stillness makes room for feelings, then it also makes room for filling. As we hold ourselves still in God's presence, refusing to self-medicate with our usual coping mechanisms of busyness and usefulness, we make room for his Spirit to fill us with life again. Perhaps you fear the feelings because you worry that they will cut you off from sensing God's presence in that still place. If so, take heart. God is absolutely capable of communicating love and hope to you, even in the midst of the darkest thoughts. It may not happen instantly, but as you develop the discipline of stillness, you will learn how to feel his strong, gentle presence beneath the tidal waves of your suffering and sorrow.

When I talk about contemplative prayer, people often ask whether it might be dangerous simply to sit in stillness. Might we be opening our minds to malign influences? Key to understanding all Christian meditation, contemplation or stillness is to realise that it's not about emptying ourselves; it's about filling ourselves – or rather, allowing ourselves to be filled with more and more of Jesus. If we want to be filled, then we need to be as unashamedly focused as Jeremiah and Mary were.

Picture yourself in a cafe, holding a jug of water that you'd like to pour into your friend's glass. If they're holding the glass in their hand, then the first thing you'll ask them to do is to keep it still. For filling to occur, there needs to be a moment of still and steady focus. The faster we move and the busier we get, the less opportunity we give God to pour his life-giving Spirit into us. Every moment we can spend in stillness is one more moment when he can fill us with himself.

Trying it

Have another go at the stillness exercise at the end of the previous section of this chapter, but this time choose a piece of your favourite music to listen to as you still yourself. Once you've settled into a comfortable, upright sitting position, begin to listen carefully to the music, noticing the feelings it evokes. Perhaps there are words that touch your soul, or textures in the instrumentation that stir something in you. Resist the temptation to make sense of any of it; just let the thoughts and feelings come and go – and stay still.

As the music finishes, reach out your hands, palms up, and imagine you're letting go of all that stirred within you as you listened. Give it back to God and ask him to fill you with more of himself.

Talking it

- What do you usually do to cope with your negative feelings, or to anaesthetise yourself from them?
- Have you ever had an experience of God's presence during a time of stillness? What happened and what surprised you most?
- Do you worry about the idea of certain feelings surfacing during a time of prayer? Which feelings would concern you most and why?

Sustaining it

Here are a few techniques that you might find helpful as you get used to feelings and fillings.

1 'Catch and release'
Some people think that stillness prayer means switching off our brains. If you've ever tried to stop thinking altogether, even for ten seconds, you'll know it's impossible. Our brains are designed to keep working all the time, and there's nothing wrong with that. The only knack we do need to learn is how not to let our brains take us on long detours that draw our focus away from God. One way to do this is to practise 'catch and release'. As a thought comes to you, whether it's about global politics, your friend's puppy or what you're going to have for dinner tonight, catch it: notice it and hold it for a few seconds, turning it into a prayer (e.g. 'Lord, thank you for the gift of food'). Then release it: let it go and give it to God. You may even find it helpful to make gestures of 'catch' and 'release' with your hands, as a sign of what you're doing in your mind.

2 Ever-present help

When feelings of sorrow or pain are strong, it is easy to think that God is at a distance, watching us impassively as we wrestle with life. In those times, it's helpful to remember that amazing story of Jesus in the boat with his disciples, living the storm with them and then calming it for them (Mark 4:35–41). No matter what feelings surface during your time of stillness, remind yourself that Jesus is right in the middle of the storm with you. He is not annoyed by your feelings, he is not ashamed of you and he is not afraid of what you're going through. He is just there, calm and peaceful, ready to give you his peace.

3 Use your pulse

One of the most ancient traditions in stillness prayer is using your own pulse as a way of stilling your body and focusing your heart and mind. Use your first two fingers to find your pulse, just above where your thumb joins your wrist, and feel the rhythm of it. Then repeat the word 'Jesus' in your mind, saying each syllable in time with a beat of your pulse. As you do this, you might find it helpful to imagine the life of Jesus flowing through your body, just as your heart is pumping blood through your veins.

Group prayer activity

Light some candles in the middle of the room and choose some gentle instrumental music to play. Invite the group to spend about ten minutes in stillness. Then invite people to share how it felt and what they learnt about themselves.

5

Action

What you do in the present – by painting, preaching, singing, sewing, praying, teaching, building hospitals, digging wells, campaigning for justice, writing poems, caring for the needy, loving your neighbour as yourself – will last into God's future. These activities are not simply ways of making the present life a little less beastly, a little more bearable, until the day when we leave it behind altogether. They are part of what we may call building for God's kingdom.

N.T. Wright, *Surprised by Hope: Rethinking heaven, the resurrection, and the mission of the church* (Harper, 2008)

Prayer beyond words
2 Kings 2:19–22; 4:38–41; 5:9–14; 6:1–7

Francis of Assisi had a habit of taking his clothes off in public. He was born in the late twelfth century to a wealthy family of cloth merchants, and as a young man he prided himself on dressing in the finest materials and the latest fashions. Then he ended up in prison for a year, and God got hold of him. As is so often the way when the divine invades our lives, Francis' relationship with God began to unpick the seams of his old priorities. Instead of loving the trappings of his glamorous life, he started to see how sharply they contrasted with the poverty of so many around him. When things make us uncomfortable, our first instinct is to take them off, and Francis took that maxim literally. On one occasion, he was passing through the town centre when he met a homeless man in rags. Moved by the man's condition and painfully aware of the fine clothes he himself was wearing, his reaction was heartfelt and full-bodied. Instead of just handing over some coins, he stripped off his top-of-the-range outfit and swapped it for the man's rags, right there in the street.

At first, Francis' father, Pietro, humoured his son's habit of donating the family wealth to those who had nothing, but eventually he lost patience. A bit of alms-giving was all well and good, but Francis had just sold a bolt of his costliest cloth and was apparently about to give the proceeds to the poor. That was a step too far, so he pursued his son to the town centre and confronted him publicly, demanding that he repay all the money he had made on the sale. What did Francis do? Did he prepare a carefully worded counterargument or take his irate father aside to resolve the situation amicably? No, he responded in that dramatic, whole-body way of his again: he stripped off all his expensive clothing, gave it back to his father, along with the money, and stood there in the street, stark naked. Fortunately, the bishop of Assisi just happened to be on hand with a cloak to cover his modesty, but I get the feeling Francis would have done it anyway, even without the episcopal intervention.

Francis' action was a masterclass in how to communicate without saying a single word, and in a world where religion was very much a matter of words, he was a breath of fresh air. His order of friars didn't live in walled-in monasteries, reciting liturgies and studying books; they travelled the highways and byways, begging for food and serving the poor. They were preachers, but Francis expected them to live out their message, right there in front of people, in a whole-body, whole-life kind of way.

Words are a priceless gift, and the ability to use them well has ensured the passing on of the Christian faith from generation to generation. Through the scriptures, the liturgies of the church and the writings of the saints, the glorious truths of God and his kingdom have made their way to us across the expanse of the years. Yet words have sometimes become too important, particularly when it comes to prayer. How often have you sat in a prayer meeting, bursting to say something to God, but you've hesitated because you're not sure if your words will be good enough? And how often have you finally plucked up the courage to speak, only to be put off again by the sheer poetic beauty of someone else's prayer? We all know that prayer is what happens in our hearts, but it's amazing how hung up we still get on what comes out of our mouths. Of course, communicating with God in words is a wonderful thing to do, but we easily forget that he understands plenty of other 'languages' too. The God who communicates with us through nature, through music, through the laughter of a baby and the touch of a friend – that God doesn't need us to stick to words when we communicate with him.

Francis was just one in a long line of people who understood that our actions can speak just as eloquently as our words. Take Elisha, for instance, a young man who suddenly shot to prominence after the strange disappearance of his mentor, the prophet Elijah. He had an inspiringly varied pallet when it came to prayer.

The trouble with being a prophet in Elisha's time was that everyone expected you to know how to say the right prayers – the kind of prayers that would rescue terrible situations. So, when the people of Jericho started dying because of a polluted water source, the most obvious course of action was to go to the prophet and get him to pray the right prayer (2 Kings 2:19–22). To the young Elisha, that must have felt like an awful lot of pressure, and I often wonder what went through his head as he contemplated what he should pray, to save the city from near-certain death. What came to him in the end was not a poetic utterance; it was an action. His prayer was to throw salt into the spring. He did speak some words at the same time, but they were more of a commentary, for the sake of those watching. Everyone present in that moment would have understood that the throwing of the salt was the prayer. And sure enough, the prayer was answered, because the spring stayed fresh from then on.

Elisha's friends must have got used to his rather physical approach to prayer. His prayer to rescue a lost axe-head was to drop a stick in the river (2 Kings 6:1–7), and his prayer to neutralise the poison in a stew was to mix flour into it (2 Kings 4:38–41). He even persuaded Naaman to wash seven times in a muddy river, as a prayer to have his leprosy healed (2 Kings 5:9–14).

How about you? Have you ever tried to pray without using words? I remember once spending time in a prayer room that was kitted out with various creative prayer activities. In one corner of the room was a mass of tangled string, and next to it was a notice outlining a few of the world's most severe injustices. The instructions were simple: just spend some time untangling the string. It was a profound moment for me. Had I tried to pray for those terrible situations in words, I would soon have got bogged down in the complexities, and my prayers would probably have felt blurred and futile, but as my fingers worked away at the tangled mess, I could connect the frustration of loosening stubborn knots with the desperation to see people set free. With each twist and tug, I was praying, and with each straightened-out piece of string, hope was stirring.

When we depend on words, our prayers can so easily become over-complicated. In a bid to try to say the best prayer, even in our own heads, we can lose touch with the simple, heartfelt longings we most need to express. When we go beyond words to actions, it forces us to be more focused and more straightforward. Francis' stripping off in public was somehow a far more eloquent message about wealth and poverty than a magazine article on the subject would have been. The young, inexperienced Elisha probably had no idea how to forge an impressive prayer about city water-purification systems, so he did something that expressed his simple, heartfelt longing – he sprinkled a well-known purifying agent into the spring. And for me, the untying of those knots felt like the most powerful prayer against injustice I have ever uttered.

Trying it

Our lives are full of activities, many of which make very good 'action prayers', if we do them prayerfully. Think of a difficult or unpleasant practical task that needs doing – something in the house or garden that needs cleaning, perhaps. Before you make a start, think of a difficult situation that you're praying for at the moment, preferably one you feel strongly about. Then, as you work, let your physical actions become your prayer for that situation. Perhaps the scrubbing of ingrained dirt expresses your longing to see forgiveness and reconciliation; perhaps the work of repairing something expresses your desire to see God rebuild broken lives; perhaps the business of weeding, digging and planting expresses your prayer to see new growth in your church.

As you do your prayer action, don't forget to listen. God will probably want to say just as much to you through that task as you want to say to him.

Talking it

- Have you ever seen someone do something with such heart and determination that it's felt more like a prayer than an action?
- Are there any practical activities in your daily life that always seem to turn into prayer?
- When we pray together at church or in our small groups, what can we do to become more active and less wordy in prayer?

Sustaining it

One of the easiest prayer actions is prayer walking. It's the simple, physical act of praying for a place by being there. Elisha may have used salt, sticks and flour, but we use our own bodies, planting our feet on the ground in places where we long to see God's kingdom come. Why not devise a prayer walk and commit to doing it regularly over the coming months?

1 Pick a place

Is there a route you walk or drive often, or is there a part of your local community you long to see transformed? That's the best place to start your rhythm of prayer walking. Each time you go to that place or follow that familiar route, travel it as an act of prayer.

2 Be the prayer

As you walk, you will probably find that all sorts of thoughts and ideas bubble up in your mind, but try to resist the temptation to make prayers out of words. This is a prayer action, so your prayer is your physical act of walking. As you take each step, imagine it's a prayer. You may want to alter your speed or your stride, depending on what your unspoken prayer is about: if the place needs peace, walk slowly and calmly; if you're longing for breakthrough, stride out purposefully; if your prayer is thankfulness and gratitude, walk with a spring in your step. Let your physical movements be the prayer.

3 Keep your eyes open

This is good advice if you want to stay safe while you're out and about, but it has another application when it comes to prayer walking. If you can communicate with God without using words, then he can do the same back to you. He uses all our senses to speak to us. His 'voice' may come to us through a sight, a taste or a texture just as much as through a sound or a thought. If you're prayer walking, he is bound to want to join in the wordless conversation, so look out for things he draws your attention to. What do you see? What might he be saying?

Doing and making
Luke 9:28–36; Matthew 14:22–33

Some years ago, we moved into a house that needed a large amount of renovation. Money being a little tight, we decided to do as much of the work ourselves as we could, and this necessitated us becoming dab hands at a whole range of tasks. We had to master painting, plastering, woodwork, cleaning, negotiating with tradesmen and the very satisfying job of demolishing things with a sledgehammer, to name but a few. I am by nature someone who enjoys stillness and silence in prayer, but if you've ever lived in a house mid-renovation, you'll know that it's difficult enough to find a chair to sit on, let alone securing a quiet hour with no drilling or hammering, so I had to become adept at action prayer. On one occasion I was doing a bit of prayer hoovering, and I fell off the side of a staircase. As I lay on the landing four feet below, having very nearly landed on the dog's bed, which would have done some serious damage to my back, I found myself musing that action prayer has a significantly higher risk factor to it than the more sedentary types I prefer.

The apostle Peter had the honour of praying with Jesus. What a masterclass, to pray with the man who was healing the sick, driving out evil spirits and generally confounding everyone's expectations of what was possible in life. It would have been an honour to watch with him in prayer, wouldn't it? Yet the gospels tell of two occasions when Peter and his friends fell asleep as their master conversed with his heavenly Father (Luke 9:32; 22:45). If you found the stillness activities in the previous chapter difficult, then take heart from Peter. He got to sit in stillness with the greatest man who ever lived, and yet he found it almost impossible, because he was an activist at heart.

Whether intentionally or not, many churches have emphasised stillness and silence as the most devout way of praying, and if you're the reflective type, this has probably suited you well. But if you're an activist, like Peter, then this may have left you feeling nothing but guilty and inadequate. Many Christians down the centuries have beaten themselves up for not being good at stillness, and many have given up on prayer altogether as a result. Yet, while stillness is an important discipline to cultivate, it's not the be-all and end-all of prayer. Perhaps you're more like Peter, and prayer comes alive for you when it's about doing or making, moving or taking action.

As Peter and his friends awoke from one of those naps, something remarkable was happening around them (Luke 9:28–36). Jesus was transfigured amid a shining cloud of glory, and he seemed to be in conversation with Moses and Elijah, who had been dead for centuries. By any standards, this was a moment for wonder. They must have been awestruck, yet Peter's reaction was not to fall face down in silent adoration. His gut reaction was to do something, so he offered to build shelters.

He often gets a bad press for that. Of course, it was a mad idea – Moses and Elijah weren't likely to be sticking around, and Jesus was hardly the type to want to sit in a booth on top of a mountain – but perhaps his offer says more about his prayer life than his theology. Perhaps he had no idea where to start in finding the right words for that sacred moment, but he longed to show his devotion, and the only thing he could think of was to do something, to make something with his hands. Had they been anywhere near a lake, perhaps he'd have offered to build each of them the finest fishing boat money could buy.

Do you ever think of your talents as a prayer language? If prayer is, at its simplest, the expression of ourselves to God and the opening of ourselves to his presence, then it makes sense that the things we love doing might just help us in that self-to-self communication.

The story is told of an elderly lady who was having trouble praying. One day, the bishop came to preach at her church, and she took him aside after the service to ask his advice. To her surprise, he asked what she most enjoyed doing. She told him she was an avid knitter, so he told her to abandon her prayer time for the next few weeks and to knit instead. When he made his return visit, several weeks later, he sought her out and asked how the prayer was going. 'Well,' she said, 'it's the oddest thing. For a few days I thought you must be mad, but then one morning I was sitting in my armchair knitting, not really thinking about anything, and suddenly I felt him there in the room with me. I have never felt that before in my life. I didn't want to stop knitting in case he left, so we just sat together while I finished the sleeve of my granddaughter's jumper. And you know, he's turned up every day since then.'

If you're really stuck with prayer, one of the best ways to get unstuck is to spend your prayer time doing something you love. Stop trying to make yourself a different shape when you pray. Stop trying to pray like others pray. Just do something that comes naturally to you – something you enjoy or something you're good at – and see what happens. The gospel writers may have been a little hard on Peter for his shelter-building suggestion, but Jesus didn't criticise him. He was his friend, so he must have known that this was Peter's best and most loving prayer. And since Jesus is your friend, too, the same goes for you. He is delighted when you communicate your love to him in your favourite language.

Another of Peter's memorable moments did take place on a lake, in the middle of the night in a howling gale (Matthew 14:22–33). Jesus was walking on the water, and Peter, being an activist, decided he needed to make sense of this bizarre situation by doing something. At Jesus' invitation, he climbed down from the boat and started to walk on the surface of the churning sea. It was a courageous stride into the unknown and the impossible, and it resulted in him experiencing the presence of Jesus in a way none of the other disciples did.

If we only ever understand prayer as a pattern of familiar habits and well-worn words, it is likely to remain a dry, dusty ritual. One of the reasons for incorporating some creativity and movement into our rhythm of prayer is that it opens us to adventure. When prayer is words, it can be predictable, even controllable. When we pray with our whole bodies, by making and doing, we make ourselves available for God to meet with us in new and surprising ways. The one we talk to suddenly becomes the one who gardens with us, knits with us and pulls us out of the waves.

Trying it

What's your hobby? Make some time in the coming week to do something you love. If you're particularly busy, your hobby may be the thing you do to wind down or switch off, but this time it's going to be an act of prayer – not switching off from the world but switching on to the presence of God. Before you begin your activity, thank God for it; it's a gift from him, after all. Then, invite him to join you in it, by his Spirit. As you do your activity, give it your best, as a sign of your love for him. Most of all, enjoy it. It's you being truly yourself, and that gives God the perfect opportunity to make his presence known in your life. He might just surprise you.

Talking it

- What could you do to make your prayer life a bit more adventurous?
- Is there a particular piece of art that feels to you like a prayer? What do you think the artist was trying to express through it?
- We're good at using our talents to do useful things in church, but how could we make more room for beauty – encouraging people to do or make beautiful things, purely as acts of prayer to the glory of God?

Sustaining it

1 Acts of beauty
Throughout the centuries, people have made beautiful things as acts of worship, quite simply because God is worth it. Craftsmen used to put exquisite artwork high up in the vaults of cathedral roofs, for instance, not because any human would ever be likely to see it, but as a prayer, honouring God with their talent. What do you do or make that is beautiful? Instead of using that talent to fill a need or help another person, why not do or make something, purely as a prayer to God?

2 Acts of blessing

We usually assume that praying for people involves formulating a few sentences about them, and then speaking them to God, either in our heads or out loud. But what if you prayed for someone through your actions instead of your words? Next time you do something for someone – make them a coffee, give them a hug or carry a heavy bag for them – let your action express to God the prayer in your heart for them.

3 Acts of justice

When it comes to confronting injustice, words can seem frustratingly ineffective. That's when actions really can speak louder than words, and many people involved in fighting for social justice find action prayer far more meaningful than spoken prayer. Is there a justice issue that you feel passionately about? Is there something you could do, not only as a protest or a gesture of support, but as a prayer? Better still, could you gather a group to take action together? Action prayer is a refreshing, liberating practice to build into your own personal prayer rhythm, but it comes to life even more when you get others involved, so why not gather a group of friends who share a passion for a particular issue in your local community, then start devising some action prayers you can do together?

Group prayer activity

Take your group on a prayer walk around your local neighbourhood. Point out places (school, park, police station, etc.) along the way that they can pray for. When you get back, talk about what you saw, heard and prayed.

- - - - - - - - -
6
- - - - - - - - -

Intercession

Intercession is truly universal work for the Christian. No place is closed to intercessory prayer: no continent, no nation, no organization, no city, no office. There is no power on earth that can keep intercession out.

Richard C. Halverson, *No Greater Power: Perspective for days of pressure*
(Multnomah Press, 1986)

Shoulder prayers
Exodus 28:6–14; Ephesians 6:18; Philippians 4:6; 1 Thessalonians 5:17; 1 Timothy 2:1–4

May 1940 was a dark month for Britain and her World War II allies. Hitler's attacks on France and Belgium had become so intense that almost 350,000 Allied troops were trapped, with nowhere to flee but into the English Channel. In fact, so desperate was their plight that the German High Command even reported, 'The British army is encircled and our troops are proceeding to its annihilation.'

But they were reckoning without prayer. King George VI called a National Day of Prayer on Sunday 26 May, and the nation responded wholeheartedly. Churches were packed; cathedrals couldn't contain the thousands who flocked there to pray, so many ended up praying in the queues outside. A great cry went up from millions of hearts, and suddenly the tables turned.

History records three miracles in the days that followed. On Monday 27 May, Hitler ordered his own troops to halt their attack, even though they were only ten miles from overwhelming the Allied forces. Historians still have no clear idea why he did this, except perhaps that he believed the Luftwaffe, his formidable air force, would be enough to disrupt any potential sea evacuation. If this was the reason, then it makes the second miracle all the more remarkable. On Tuesday 28 May, the most violent storm in a generation blew up over Flanders, completely grounding the aircraft Hitler had been relying on. The storm cover also allowed the remaining Allied troops to walk the ten miles or so to the Dunkirk beach with no fear of being attacked from the air.

And then, on Wednesday 29 May, despite the storm raging just a few miles away, a miraculous calm settled over the English Channel. For the next few days, the sea was like a mill pond, allowing almost 1,000 boats of all shapes and sizes to rescue the embattled soldiers and bring them to safe shores. A week earlier, the best Churchill and his War Cabinet could hope for was the saving of perhaps 30,000 lives, but in the end, over ten times that number were rescued.

The only possible explanation for the 'Miracle of Dunkirk', as it has become known, is intercessory prayer. It was arguably the most powerful weapon used during World War II, and it wasn't wielded by experts with special training; it was wielded by millions of ordinary people. With a tool as powerful as that in our hands, it makes sense to learn a little more about it.

The word 'intercede' comes from two Latin words: *cedere*, meaning 'to go' or 'to move', and *inter*, meaning 'between'. So to be an intercessor is to be a go-between. Intercession is bringing people and situations to God, bringing God to people and situations, and doing all of it through prayer.

The people of Israel had designated go-betweens, called priests. Their role was to carry the needs of the people to God and to carry the blessing of God to the people. In the book of Exodus, we read about the garments that the high priest was required to wear, and they beautifully depict the job God was entrusting to him (Exodus 28:6–14). The vestments included stones, which were engraved with the names of the twelve tribes of Israel, because the high priest was to carry his people into the presence of God each year, holding them before him in prayer. But he didn't just wear one set of engraved stones, he wore two: one set on his shoulders and one over his heart.

If you have ever spent time praying for anything or anyone, then you'll know that intercession feels very different, depending on who or what it is that you're carrying to God in prayer. Sometimes it's the easiest thing in the world, because the things we're praying for are things that matter deeply to us, and that we could probably keep praying about for hours. Other times it is hard work. We know it's important to bring them to God, but it feels dry and draining. I take heart from those priestly garments, because it's as though God knew that carrying people and situations to him in prayer would sometimes be like releasing a deep cry from the heart, and at other times it would be more like lugging a load on our shoulders.

We're going to come back to those 'heart prayers' in the next section, but let's spend a moment thinking about the 'shoulder prayers' – the things we know God is asking us to pray about, but which we find more of a duty than a joy.

> I urge you, first of all, to pray for all people. Ask God to help them; intercede on their behalf, and give thanks for them. Pray this way for kings and all who are in authority so that we can live peaceful and quiet lives marked by godliness and dignity. This is good and pleases God our Saviour, who wants everyone to be saved and to understand the truth.
> 1 TIMOTHY 2:1–4 (NLT)

The apostle Paul was a man who most definitely believed in the importance of intercessory prayer, and one of the words you'll find most often in his teaching on it is the word 'all'. We're to pray for all people (1 Timothy 2:1); we're to pray in all situations (Philippians 4:6); we're to pray on all occasions with all kinds of prayers (Ephesians 6:18); in fact, we're to pray continually (1 Thessalonians 5:17). It can make you weary just thinking about it, can't it? But Paul had good cause to set the bar so high. He spent his life taking the good news of Jesus to places where no one had ever heard it before, and he knew that no amount of persuasive preaching or impressive supernatural signs would change people's hearts. That was a miracle that only prayer could bring about. If the kingdom of our God is to reshape the kingdoms of this world, it will be because his people soak every aspect of society in prayer.

The good news is, we don't have to do the 'all' on our own. It's not your job to pray for everyone everywhere. That's something we do together, as the whole church. Yet it is important for us to broaden our prayer scope. It's all too easy to get stuck in praying for the things that matter most to us. The first challenge is to step out of your prayer echo chamber, and ask God to show you which new prayer responsibilities he'd like you to shoulder, for the sake of his kingdom. There are people and situations out there that might never get prayed for if you don't notice them and carry them to him.

Some of the most faithful intercessors I know are avid readers of the local newspaper. They make it their business to get informed about their local community, so that they know what needs praying for. Others make a habit of following local politics – knowing the names of their councillors and the issues under discussion at council meetings – so that they can pray in an informed way. Others commit to praying for missionaries and the countries where they serve, or for those working to address a particular social justice issue.

The crucial thing is to realise that this kind of prayer takes time and discipline. When you pray for a loved one who's ill, you already know the situation inside out, and you can pray from the heart, anywhere, anytime. When you're praying 'shoulder prayers', you're praying for

2. Worship

Praise — most psalms of David's

Psalms ___ David/Samuel was

writing, viewing the landscape

that he was encountering God in

the beauty of creation and he

was "delighted" + "will praise.

Ps 18 Praise again, one of the most

Famous psalms,

Spirit of Gratitude (praise)

Ps 51

people you don't necessarily see often, or for things you don't know much about. Either way, it takes time and you need to be intentional about it. If you're praying for people in your extended family, for instance, or for the members of your church, then you need to stop and think about each person, and pray a specific prayer of blessing over them. If you're praying for a situation you don't know much about, you need to schedule time to get informed, and to pray about what you've discovered. We can all say a two-sentence prayer for our local council, for instance, but prayer is most effective when it is specific, and that means taking time to research and to pray through the details.

Another miracle was reported during the Dunkirk evacuation. As the Allied troops waited to be rescued, German forces were raining gunfire down on them, yet surprisingly few were killed. One man even testified to having laid flat on the ground, fully expecting to die in a hail of bullets, only to find, when he stood up, that though bullet holes marked the outline of his body on the sand, not one bullet had hit him.

As the nation cried to God for deliverance, only a few people would have known the details of how the evacuation was to be affected, but I am certain that some of them must have been praying people. They would have given thought to what was about to happen, to the dangers those soldiers would face, and they were able to pray through every aspect of the operation in great detail. I am convinced that Dunkirk's beach was a safer place for the Allied troops as a result of those faithful praying people.

Trying it

Choose a current news story to pray about. First, take time to do some research: read a few articles and write down what you learn. Then, use your notes to inform your prayer. Pray for each person involved by name; think about how they might be feeling; pray for the circumstances that need to change or the issues that need to be resolved. Bring that situation before God, taking time to pray detailed, specific prayers.

Talking it

- Have you ever seen God answer prayer in a miraculous way?
- What do you find easy to pray for, and what are the things you find more difficult to get motivated to pray for?
- Why do you think intercessory prayer makes such a difference? Why doesn't God just get on and do what needs doing, even when we don't pray?

Sustaining it

1 Devise a system
There will always be a small number of people you carry in your heart, and it will be easy to pray for them, but if you want to be faithful and consistent in praying for everyone God has placed in your care (extended family, work colleagues, church members, etc.), then you will need to devise a system for making sure you pray through them methodically. The easiest way is simply to make a list and to work your way through it, praying for seven or eight people each day.

2 Join a mailing list
Is there a particular ministry you know God is asking you to commit to praying for? If so, sign up for their newsletter, and make sure you stop to read and digest it when it arrives. You may even want to print it out and leave it somewhere you'll see it, so that you remember to pray.

3 Get a map
One of the best ways to pray for your local community, the nation or the world is with a map. Having the different areas set out in front of you in visual form can help you to pray more methodically. You might even like to put your hand on the area you're praying for, or light a tea light and put it on the place you want to bring to God.

Heart prayers
Exodus 28:15–30; Romans 8:26, 34; Galatians 4:19;
Philippians 1:8; Colossians 4:12; 2 Timothy 1:3–4

I used to be The Salvation Army's national prayer coordinator, and one of my tasks each year was to run a prayer tent at our annual ROOTS Conference. The conference always had a theme, but each year we would also include a social justice focus, as a way of raising awareness, raising funds and raising prayer. One year, the social justice focus was human trafficking, and I confess I was struggling to engage with it. I could pray about it as a 'shoulder prayer', researching the complex issues and formulating prayers that were specific and accurate, but I knew that, if I were to help others to connect with the seriousness of this evil trade, I needed to take it to heart.

The shift came one Saturday morning when I was sitting in my kitchen, eating my breakfast and listening to the radio. A journalist was telling the story of a man who worked undercover to track down people traffickers, putting himself in grave danger to expose their networks and rescue their victims. His name was Geoff – that's all the journalist could say, for fear of endangering him further. By the end of the report, I was crying. I was crying because suddenly human trafficking and all its terrible implications had become a little more real to me; and I was crying as a prayer for Geoff – a man willing to risk his life to see justice done. Throughout the conference, if ever I struggled to engage with the social justice focus, I would simply think of Geoff.

Israel's high priest wore the names of the twelve tribes over his heart (Exodus 28:15–30). Whereas the shoulder pieces simply had all twelve tribal names engraved on two pieces of onyx, the heart piece had each tribe's name engraved on a separate stone, and each stone was of immense value. The high priest would not have been allowed to enter the holy of holies without both the shoulder and the heart pieces. He was the intercessor, the go-between, who was to shoulder spiritual responsibility for his people, but who was also to carry them in his heart, as precious and beautiful in God's sight.

If 'shoulder prayers' are a form of intercession that primarily engages our minds, then 'heart prayers' are a form of intercession that is more likely to engage our emotions. I knew that my praying about human trafficking had become a heart prayer when Geoff and his work brought me to tears. Heart prayers aren't difficult to form; they well up from within us, and they often find expression in our bodies as well as our words.

The apostle Paul knew all about this kind of praying. His letters are peppered with references to him praying for his readers, but there are a few that stand out as having a more emotional tone.

> Timothy, I thank God for you... Night and day I constantly remember you in my prayers. I long to see you again, for I remember your tears as we parted. And I will be filled with joy when we are together again.
>
> 2 TIMOTHY 1:3–4 (NLT)

Timothy was like a son to Paul, and that affection coloured how Paul prayed for him. If you pray for something 'night and day', it's because you can't get it out of your head; you lose sleep over it. That was the case for several of the people and communities Paul wrote to. He told the Philippians that he held them in his heart, and that he longed for them with 'the affection of Christ Jesus' (Philippians 1:8, ESV). He told the Galatians that he was in the 'anguish of childbirth' for them (Galatians 4:19, ESV). These weren't tidy, arm's-length prayers; these were inconvenient, messy, costly prayers that came from deep within Paul's being.

What is your heart prayer at the moment? Is there a person or situation that is keeping you awake at night because you care so deeply about them or it? People often tell me they worry that God might be bored of hearing them go on and on about the same thing, but let me reassure you: that prayer you can't seem to stop praying – it doesn't annoy God; to him, it is one of the beautiful, precious stones that you carry over your heart, and he receives it with special tenderness, because he knows how much it matters to you.

Paul also recognised that some prayers are so deep in us that we simply can't articulate them. If you have ever felt truly heartbroken about a situation, or if you have shared even a tiny bit of someone else's grief, then you'll know that feeling. It's not that you don't want to pray; it's that you have no words. In one of his most poignant prayer pictures, Paul describes what happens in these moments:

> In the same way the Spirit also helps our weakness; for we do not know how to pray as we should, but the Spirit Himself intercedes for us with groanings too deep for words.
> ROMANS 8:26 (NASB)

Your shoulders can probably bear a lot of weight, but your heart is more fragile, and sometimes it simply gets overloaded. That's when the Holy Spirit comes to help you pray, gathering up all that is most precious to you, and lifting it to the Father for you when you have no words left. And just a few verses further on, Paul tells us that Jesus is busy interceding for us, too (Romans 8:34). The Father has invited you to take up the ministry of intercession – carrying the needs and pains of others to him in prayer – but he has not left you to do it alone. At least two members of the Trinity are sharing the load with you.

Paul has left us one more prayer picture that helps us understand what heart prayer might feel like. In a passing comment in his letter to the Colossians, he refers to his friend Epaphras as 'always wrestling in prayer' for them (Colossians 4:12). Heart prayer can feel a lot like wrestling, as we keep crying out to God for breakthrough. It's important to say that we're not wrestling with God. We're not trying to persuade him with the sheer vociferousness of our praying. Prayer is never about persuading God, but it is sometimes about partnering with him in seeing a difficult situation resolved. Could he do it without our prayers? Yes, of course he could. But he has chosen to include us in his work, and intercession is one of the most important means by which we partner with him in establishing his kingdom in our world.

Has God given you a cause to fight for in prayer? Is there something that you feel so strongly about that praying for it almost feels like a physical pressure inside of you? Be encouraged – that's a heart prayer, and God honours you for it. He will also give you supernatural strength to keep going until the praying is done. Many intercessors find they can wrestle in prayer for hours over a heart prayer like that. And then a moment will come when the Holy Spirit stands you down, because the work is done. When you feel that nudge, give thanks to God and have a good long rest.

Trying it

If you have a heart prayer, then the chances are you're constantly lifting it to God, but it's still important to set aside time to focus on it in prayer. So choose the situation that most preoccupies your prayers, and then begin to pour out your heart to God. You may want to do this in words, with tears or even with groans from the depths of yourself. You may want to find a body position that expresses how you feel – kneeling, lying face-down or pacing the room, for instance. Whatever you do, be completely honest. Don't try to pray well-informed, accurate prayers; don't try to form theologically sound requests; just pour out your heart to the one who sees the depths of you.

Talking it

- Are you carrying a heart prayer at the moment? How long have you been carrying it, and have you seen God answer it in any way yet?
- Have you ever been aware of the Holy Spirit helping you to pray when you weren't able to? What happened, and what was it like?

- When we pray together, either in church or in small groups, prayer can often feel rather cerebral. What might we do to release a bit more heart prayer in our meetings?

Sustaining it

1 Borrow some words
When it's hard to find words to express the prayers that come from the deepest place within you, it can help to borrow someone else's. Find a book of prayers, or search the internet, and look for a prayer, passage or poem that seems to echo the cry of your own heart. Keep it to hand so you can read it often.

2 Hold a promise
Heart prayers can be particularly painful, because they're the ones that grieve us most when we don't see answers. Ask God to give you a promise from scripture that you can call to mind whenever you feel discouraged. It doesn't need to be a promise about the outcome of your praying, just a promise about the goodness of the one you pray to.

3 Enlarge your heart
Our heart prayers are often about those we love, or situations we are close to. Yet there's a world out there that desperately needs our heartfelt intercession. Is there something that God is asking you to take to heart – a nation or people-group, perhaps, or an issue such as people trafficking? When you want to get informed about a shoulder prayer, it's good to read facts; when you want to connect with a heart prayer, you need to read stories. Find the stories of people who are living the reality of the situation you're going to pray for, and let their experiences stir your emotions.

Group prayer activity

Find some Bible verses that are designed to be coloured in and put them in the middle of the room. Ask the group to get into pairs and to share with each other a heart prayer they're praying at the moment. Then invite them all to choose a Bible verse, colour it in and give it to their partner as an encouragement in their praying.

7

Strategy

There is a general kind of praying which fails for lack of
precision. It is as if a regiment of soldiers should all fire off
their guns anywhere. Possibly somebody would be killed, but
the majority of the enemy would be missed.

Charles Haddon Spurgeon, *Day by Day with C.H. Spurgeon* (Kregel Publications, 1990)

Prayerful planning
Nehemiah 1:1—2:9; 4:1–18

For the past few years, I've been working as a prayer consultant.
The job takes me into all kinds of different situations, but the ones
that excite me most are those involving some measure of strategy.
It might be a leadership team asking me to help them develop their
church's prayer life. It might be walking alongside a newly founded
organisation, helping them to weave prayer into every aspect of
their work. It might be working with an ecumenical group, devising
a prayer strategy that will impact their local community. No matter
how big or small the strategy, this kind of work fascinates and
inspires me, because I have the kind of mind that enjoys analysing
things and seeing how they fit together.

Years ago, the prayer group and the strategy team rarely crossed
paths, but as our hunger for prayer has increased, more and more
people are recognising the value of mixing prayer and project man-
agement. Nowadays, you are almost as likely to find spreadsheets

and architect's drawings at a prayer meeting as you are to find candles and Bibles. We are slowly debunking the myth that prayer meetings are for 'spiritual' people, whereas planning meetings are for pragmatic people who get things done. It's a particularly damaging myth because it has led many to conclude that their love of logical thinking and problem-solving means they're not suited to the work of prayer. What's more, it has left many a vitally important project without prayer support, because the prayer group haven't understood how to pray effectively for it.

Our world badly needs people who can use their minds to apply the power of prayer in strategic ways, and one such man was Nehemiah. He lived about a century after the Israelites had begun to return from exile in Babylon, and though the temple had been rebuilt and the city repopulated, its walls were still in ruins. Despite all kinds of obstacles and opposition, the people succeeded in restoring the whole city wall in just 52 days, thanks to Nehemiah's strategic leadership. His story is a fascinating read because it demonstrates how one of the most impressive reconstruction efforts in history could not have happened without prayer.

I'm guessing you don't have a city wall to rebuild, but you certainly have things you need to get done. We often keep 'doing' and 'praying' in separate boxes. We might ask God to bless the things we need to do, but that's as far as the connection goes. Yet prayer should permeate everything we do. Our tasks, projects, plans and visions need to be saturated in prayer, and that's what Nehemiah was so good at.

Nehemiah served in the royal court of Babylon, so he had no idea what was going on in Jerusalem until his brother came to see him. When he heard how bad things were, he must have been keen to start working out a solution, but the first thing he did was to take all the information he'd gathered into the place of prayer. He didn't come up with a solution and then ask God to rubber-stamp it; he didn't sit in God's presence, waiting for a solution to drop out of the sky;

he drew near to God to think prayerfully and to pray thoughtfully. And as he did that, the Holy Spirit brought insight from God's own mind, showing him all that he needed to see (Nehemiah 1:1–11). By the time he got up from his mourning and fasting, he had a deep and complete understanding of why he was going to rebuild that city wall.

If you're making a plan, then it's worth starting where Nehemiah started. Come to God in prayer, but don't leave all your insights at the door. The information you've already received is a gift from God, and so is your ability to process that information and to devise a way forward, so come to him with your mind full and your thoughts sparking. Just don't rush off into action until you've given him a chance to add his thoughts to yours.

Nehemiah's prayer is fascinating because he prayed as though he were one of the people who had brought about Jerusalem's downfall, even though it happened long before he was born. It's as though his time in prayer gave him insight into the complex layers of rebellion and wrongdoing that had brought about that terrible destruction in the first place, and that insight shaped many of the decisions he made throughout the rebuild. If you get God's perspective before you start, then not only will the plan be a good one, but your approach to it will be good, too. When I work with churches to create prayer strategies that will help transform a local community, we usually spend time researching to find out what harmful or damaging things have been done in the name of Christianity in the past. It's partly so we can pray for healing of any lingering wounds, but it's also so that we can choose not to make those mistakes again, as we venture out into new plans and schemes. Prayer is the place where our perspective broadens and our understanding deepens. It's the place where God's Spirit shows us what we need to see. Make sure you don't skip that crucial stage.

Not all of Nehemiah's prayer was time-consuming, though. When the king put him on the spot by asking why he was sad, he suddenly had to find the courage to ask for some pretty big favours, and that's when he deployed what we now call an 'arrow prayer' (Nehemiah 2:1–9). He simply threw a quick plea for help in God's direction and plunged in with his requests. Utterly miraculously, Artaxerxes agreed to every single one.

If you're the type who gets caught up in getting a job done and only manages the odd arrow prayer when things get tricky, take heart from Nehemiah. God loves the way you get absorbed in what you're doing; he loves the way your mind whirs as you weigh things up and move things forward. He made you that way and he isn't asking you to change, but he may be asking you to remember that you didn't leave him behind when you left the place of prayer. He walks through the day with you, his mind whirs even faster than yours and he is available to be called upon with an arrow prayer whenever you need a bit of supernatural assistance.

Once a project really gets underway, it's all too easy to leave prayer behind, but that's not a mistake Nehemiah made. Prayer was an essential part of his plan throughout. Successfully executing a strategy means being able to see problems before they arise, and his reliance on prayer meant that he got ample warning from the Spirit when things were about to go wrong. He knew when fear and discouragement were setting in, and he immediately turned everyone's attention to God in prayer (Nehemiah 4:1–18). Yet he didn't just tell them all to down tools and hold a lengthy prayer vigil. The work needed to continue, so he found ways to keep them praying and working at the same time. He equipped them to defend themselves, posted guards to keep them safe and stirred their courage by praying with them and urging them to 'remember the Lord' (Nehemiah 4:14).

What does it look like for you to weave prayer and work together, as you get your plan or project underway? There's no right or wrong answer, but it's worth coming up with a way to keep prayer at the heart of your strategy. The answer may be very practical: I know people who add prayer times to their task schedules and prayer topics to their spreadsheets. Or it may be more about changing your perception of God: not thinking of him as the boss to whom you report at the end of the day, but as the master you're apprenticed to. Like any good master, he works alongside you, sharing the joys and the frustrations, and helping you get the job done.

Trying it

One of the best ways to plan prayerfully is to break your project down into two lists. The first is your to-do list, and includes all the things that you and others will need to do to bring the plan to reality. The other is the to-pray list, and includes all the things you need God to do in order for the plan to be successful – all the impossible things that you can't make happen in your own strength.

Don't worry if you think you don't have any impressive projects to plan. Every day can be a project, so why not start by thinking about what you want to achieve today, and then make your to-do list and your to-pray list?

Talking it

- Too often, prayer gets added to projects as an afterthought, but have you ever been part of a project that really did have prayer as a key component?
- Have you ever prayed an arrow prayer?
- Is there a disconnect between those who do and those who pray in your church? If so, what would help those two groups work more closely together?

Sustaining it

1 Goal-setting
Use a journal or notes app to keep track of your project in prayer. Make a note of each goal you've set, and what you need God to do for

that goal to be accomplished. Then start praying. Remember to tick things off when he answers, because that will encourage you along the way.

2 Prayerful research

When you're planning a project or devising a strategy, it's worth being well informed. God has given you a mind that can process information, and he means you to use it, so get into the habit of prayerful research. As you search for information relevant to your project, have an ear open to the whisper of the Spirit. He may point you to a document to read, or suggest a particular word or phrase for you to search on the internet. Practise following those nudges. You may get it wrong and end up down a few dead ends, but you'll become more used to it in time.

3 Involve others

Before he started work, Nehemiah took a few people on a tour of the broken-down walls. He didn't tell them why; he obviously just wanted the benefit of their wisdom. Inviting people to share their wisdom in this way can be a helpful thing to do while you're in the process of devising a new plan. You may not have walls to walk around, but talk to other people about the situation you want to address, and ask them for their thoughtful, prayerful opinions. Nehemiah gained a small bunch of committed supporters for his endeavour, and you might too.

Prayerful persevering
Mark 8:22–25; 9:14–29; Luke 11:5–13; 18:1–8

A long time ago, I read a book and I had a dream. The book was Pete Greig and Dave Roberts' *Red Moon Rising* (Kingsway, 2004), and the dream was to start a 'boiler room' prayer community in the city where I live. As I closed the book, I began to make my plans. In my mind's eye I could see a group of people who prayed and shared life together; I could see a place for people to find support and friendship; I could see a community with a heart beating for prayer, mission and justice, right in the centre of the city. With hindsight, I'm glad God never mentioned how long the dream would take to come to fruition. It was about ten years and two months later that the Canterbury Boiler Room community first opened the door to our little prayer shop.

Like Nehemiah's wall-building project, the journey has been a blend of planning, hard work and prayer, but it has also been a lesson in how to pray something through to completion. I assumed setting up a prayer community was such a good idea that it would be simple – every prayer we prayed would get answered and every obstacle would slide neatly aside as we rolled out this brilliant vision. How wrong I was! It turns out that even a prayer community takes a lot of prayer to get off the ground.

If you've got a vision, a project or just a lot of things you need to get done, then it's worth learning to make prayer part of your strategy, as Nehemiah did, but it's also worth learning how to persevere in prayer. You never know how long things might take or how hard they might get. Perseverance in prayer is something Jesus taught about a lot during his ministry on earth, so where better to start our learning?

In a culture that has become all too familiar with easy fixes and instant gratification, it is worth noting that Jesus never taught prayer as something that could be ticked off in one easy step. When he told his disciples they should ask, seek and knock (Luke 11:9–10), the verbs he used were in the present continuous tense: he was telling them to keep on asking, keep on seeking and keep on knocking.

Prayer isn't a combination lock, giving us access to everything we want, provided we get it right. Prayer is the thread that holds us in constant communion with God. We keep praying because we keep needing him; we keep praying because our visions, projects and plans will always need to be infused with his creative presence. If he keeps urging us to more and more prayer, it's not because he's needy or greedy; it's because we are infinitely less without him, and nothing we do will be as effective if he's not in it.

But keeping hold of that thread of prayer isn't easy. We forget; we get discouraged; things happen to block our way; and before we know it, we're going it alone. Jesus told the story of a widow who had a project of sorts (Luke 18:1–8). She needed justice, and she had gone to the judge to request his help, but he had cruelly palmed her off. Nothing daunted, she just kept on asking. It may not sound like a story about prayer, but Luke tells us that Jesus told it to teach his disciples that they should always pray and never give up. So what is it about the widow's persistence that teaches us something about prayer?

Jesus wanted his listeners to spot the difference between God and circumstances. The judge in the story was a circumstance. He happened to be the one with jurisdiction in the widow's community and he happened to be unkind. Life will always put obstacles in our way, but that shouldn't stop us praying. We often get discouraged when things don't work out. We wonder if it's God's way of telling us that our plans are wrong or our projects don't have his blessing, but that's not what the story of the widow teaches. The moral of her story is that circumstances happen, but they're not God and they do not have the final word. Persistence means you keep on praying, no matter what happens to dampen your resolve. If you're encountering some obstacles in the things you're seeking to achieve at the moment, don't stop praying, and don't throw your plans up in the air. Keep on asking, and the all-compassionate judge will bring things to the best conclusion.

Jesus told another story about persistence in prayer, but this time the blockage wasn't an unjust judge; it was a friend (Luke 11:5–8). He asked his listeners to imagine a visitor turning up on their doorstep when the larder was empty. In a culture that valued hospitality, that would have been a profoundly awkward and dishonouring situation, and it would have been perfectly normal to knock on a friend's door to ask for help. Only this friend wasn't helpful.

If the widow's story highlights the contrast between God and circumstances, then this story highlights the contrast between God and people. This was no random man appointed to be judge in the village; this was a friend – someone who should have been supportive – getting in the way of something important. The people around you may well be the greatest source of frustration when you're trying to realise a vision or complete a project, but the solution is not to abandon them, manipulate them or ride roughshod over them. The solution is to keep praying. Jesus told the story of the grumpy friend to remind his listeners of the goodness and kindness of God (Luke 11:11–13). When people are driving you mad, the answer is prayer. When people seem to be in your way, the answer is prayer. Go unceasingly to the one who is more gentle, more generous and more gracious than even the most wonderful of fathers. He will give you all you need to keep going. He loves you, and he loves the people who are frustrating you, so he is perfectly placed to do the best for all of you. And he may even inspire your friends to help you out in the end.

Jesus didn't just teach about persistence in prayer; he also practised it. If you ever feel like you've got something wrong because your prayers weren't answered first-time, then take heart from the story in Mark 8:22–25. When Jesus healed, it was always a moment of connection between him and the Father – it was always prayer – and in this story it was action prayer. He prayed once, putting saliva on to the man's eyes, but the result was incomplete, so he simply went back and did it again. The key to perseverance is to know when you just need to keep going. Emotions have a habit of short-circuiting prayer. Discouragement tells us to stop; self-doubt tells us we're on the wrong track; hopelessness tells us it'll never happen. Maybe Jesus had all those feelings in that moment, but he didn't act on them. He just kept praying.

Your mind has three main operations: it handles your emotions; it handles your intellect, where logical, rational thinking happens; and it handles your will, which makes decisions and sees things through to completion. Perseverance in prayer is the work of the will, ably assisted by the intellect. When emotions threaten to derail your praying, use your intellect to remind yourself of what God has asked you to accomplish, and use your will to resolve again that you won't stop until it is done.

Finally, Jesus knew when he needed to up the ante in prayer. After a mountaintop prayer time, he found his disciples trying to drive out an evil spirit from a child. When they asked him why it hadn't worked, his answer was prayer (Mark 9:14–29). Given that they'd probably been praying throughout, it must have seemed like an odd answer, but he clearly meant a different intensity of prayer. In fact, some manuscripts record him as saying, 'prayer and fasting' (Mark 9:29).

There are times when we need to turn the heat up in prayer to see our visions and plans come to fruition. If simple persistence doesn't seem to be shifting things, then you may need to switch up into another gear. Identify the specific issue where breakthrough is needed, ask some friends or colleagues to commit to praying alongside you and then make that issue the focus of your intercession for the coming weeks, until you see a change or until God tells you to stop. You may even want to fast.

Trying it

Persevering prayer is the practice of praying for the same thing many times over. Think of a vision or project you're involved in, choose one aspect of it that needs prayer, and write a three-sentence prayer about it. Then read that prayer at least three times a day for the next week. Notice how it feels to pray the same thing over and over again. What stops you doing it, and what helps you keep going?

Talking it

- Why do you think Jesus' prayer for the blind man didn't work the first time (Mark 8:22–25)?
- Have you ever prayed for the same thing for many years? If so, what was it and how long did you pray (or have you been praying)?
- Have you ever done anything else in life that called for perseverance? What lessons did you learn that you could apply to prayer?

Sustaining it

1 Beat the boredom
Perseverance in prayer is all the more difficult if you are prone to boredom. You may be praying the same prayer again and again, but you don't have to do it in the same way. If you've written the prayer from the 'Trying it' section, think of creative ways to pray it differently each time. You could pray it in different locations, for instance, or use different body postures while you pray. You could sing it, shout it, dance it or draw it.

2 Remember the goodness of God
Perseverance in prayer is harder when you doubt God's goodness. Jesus taught that the Father who loves you will not give you snakes and scorpions when you're asking for fish and eggs (Luke 11:11–13). He may not give you exactly what you want when you want it, but he is working for your good at all times. That is a helpful thing to call to mind when prayer has become a long haul.

3 Encourage yourself
History is littered with stories of people who have persevered in prayer and realised their dreams. If you're feeling discouraged, seek out some stories to renew your faith.

Group prayer activity

Give each member of the group a luggage tag. Invite everyone to write on their tag a vision or project they're praying for, then put all the tags in a dish. Each time you meet, invite everyone to take a tag (not their own) and take it home for the week, so they can support that project in prayer.

- - - - - - - -

8

- - - - - - - -

Restoration

Tell God all that is in your heart, as one unloads one's heart, its pleasures and its pains, to a dear friend. Tell God your troubles, that God may comfort you… talk to God of your temptations, that God may shield you from them: show God the wounds of your heart, that God may heal them. If you thus pour out all your weaknesses, needs, troubles, there will be no lack of what to say. Talk out of the abundance of the heart, without consideration say just what you think. Blessed are they who attain to such familiar, unreserved intercourse with God.

François Fénelon, quoted in Neil T. Anderson, *Liberating Prayer: Finding freedom by connecting with God* (Harvest House, 2012)

Inner healing
Mark 10:46–52; Luke 8:43–48

I started working for The Salvation Army in 2001, as National Prayer Coordinator. We were midway through a year of non-stop prayer in partnership with the 24-7 Prayer movement, and the atmosphere was remarkable. There was such a hunger to go deeper with God. Almost every day my inbox would fill up with messages from people wanting teaching on prayer.

We were a tiny team, so in the end, instead of trying to meet the need ourselves, we decided to train up a taskforce of 'prayer leaders' who could help us answer the numerous invitations we were getting. The 'prayer school', as we called it, started in autumn 2004 and was set to run for a year.

We all got far more than we bargained for that year. I did indeed organise some training for a keen bunch of praying folk, who have since gone on to teach prayer in all kinds of different places, but that was the least of it. We became friends, and some of those who walk closest to me today, some 15 years on, are people who did that prayer school with me. We went on to serve together, running prayer venues at Salvation Army events, doing training weekends together and partnering in prayer to see amazing breakthroughs in our churches and local communities. But the other thing I think they'd all tell you, if you asked them, is that we also got unpicked at the seams. The deeper we went with God, the more he unearthed in us, and our lives have certainly been colourful places ever since. Some of us have battled depression, some have weathered real crises of faith and some have had to confront intensely painful things from their past. We have all found ourselves unable to ignore the wounds we carry, and we have all had to recognise our need for inner healing.

It doesn't sound like a great advert for prayer, does it? But it would be disingenuous of me not to mention that, if you intend to pursue God in prayer, you may find that he uncovers some unexpected things in you. To pray consistently is to welcome the work of the Holy Spirit into the deepest parts of yourself, and that can be messy. I suppose it's logical, isn't it? If I were to visit a cobbler wearing shoes that were falling apart, I'd expect her to offer to fix them for me. If I intend to spend time with Yahweh Rapha, 'the Lord who heals' (Exodus 15:26), then I should expect him to see my wounds and to offer his healing.

That's exactly what happened for many of the people who met Jesus. Of course, most of the stories we have in the gospels are about physical healing, because that's the easiest type to see, but Jesus' healing tended to go deeper than the body. What he did in the physical realm was often a signpost to a deeper work.

That was true for both Bartimaeus (Mark 10:46–52) and the woman with menstrual problems (Luke 8:43–48). On the face of it, their healings were physical, but if we look more closely, we see the restoration of two people who lived as outsiders in their communities – people who would have been treated as subnormal and who probably suffered shame and self-hatred every day. It's faith-building to read about the miracles Jesus did in their bodies, but it's heart-strengthening to reflect on how his treatment of them healed wounds that no one in the crowds could have seen.

Have you ever noticed how many of Jesus' healing miracles happened in crowds? Of course, that's partly because he was always surrounded by so many people, but I wonder if it had another layer of meaning to it. The woman with menstrual problems had no intention of talking to Jesus. She didn't even want him to see her, so 'she came up behind him and touched the edge of his cloak' (Luke 8:44). She was healed, and surely that was enough, wasn't it? But God will never let a crowd hide an individual. Jesus knew a miracle had happened, but he also knew the healing wasn't complete until he interacted with the person. So he stopped everything in its tracks. He was on the way somewhere, but he held everyone up because it was supremely important to give her his full attention. And right there in front of hundreds of people, the woman whom everyone had avoided and shunned for years was noticed, welcomed, loved and healed.

Bartimaeus couldn't make his way through the crowd to Jesus, because he couldn't see where he was, but Jesus still stopped for him. Given how packed the road out of Jericho was, it might have been more efficient for Jesus to heal him from a distance, but that wasn't really his way, so he called him through the crowd for a face-to-face encounter (Mark 10:49).

God himself has noticed you. To him you are not a person in a crowd. You are precious beyond measure, and he loves your company. If he is talking to you about prayer – if he is calling you to make it a bigger part of your life – it's not because he thinks you should do better or work harder. It's first and foremost because he wants to draw you close and heal you.

Jesus was more than willing to meet the woman and Bartimaeus, but they also needed to be brave. There were things they needed to do – things that took great courage. For Bartimaeus, it was a determination to keep on shouting, no matter how many people told him to be quiet. For the woman, it was a determination to reach out her hand and touch Jesus, even though she knew her condition meant that her touch might make him unclean. But they were both desperate, and when you're desperate, courage comes more easily.

Inner healing is not for the faint-hearted; my prayer-school friends and I have learnt that over the years. Discovering there are unhealed wounds in you is scary, and it is all too easy to back away from prayer at that point, to keep God at arm's length. It takes courage to keep drawing near to him. It takes courage to keep stepping out from the busyness of life – which so often anaesthetises us from inner pain – and to sit with him while his Spirit touches our most tender places. It takes courage, but we would all tell you it's worth the risk. Sometimes healing doesn't look like we expect it to, but it is always better than the alternative.

As a blind person myself, I particularly love the story of Bartimaeus, and my favourite part is where Jesus asked him what he wanted (Mark 10:51). I imagine everyone in the crowd thinking, 'That's obvious, isn't it?', but Jesus took nothing for granted. This was Bartimaeus' life and Jesus accorded him the respect of letting him choose what to ask for.

Being in God's presence in prayer is definitely the starting place for healing, and he will have no qualms about showing us the wounds he wants to heal, but he is not in the business of riding roughshod over our free will. He will always leave it up to us to ask him for the healing we'd like him to do in us.

As healing was completed in the woman and in Bartimaeus, the word Jesus used for both of them was 'faith'. When we're asking for healing, we need to have faith. Faith isn't the hyped-up, triumphalist delusion that if we say all the right words then the formula will work and we'll be healed. Faith is simply trusting Jesus above everything else, and craving his company.

> Jesus said, 'Daughter, you took a risk trusting me, and now you're healed and whole. Live well, live blessed!'
> LUKE 8:48 (MSG)

Every time you turn your face towards Jesus in prayer, you are doing what both the woman and Bartimaeus did: you are touching his cloak, and you are calling for his mercy. Whether you know your wounds, or you just know you want more of him, Jesus has felt your touch, has heard your voice and has stopped to meet you. And now you're in the best place to be healed.

Trying it

Is God drawing your attention to an area of your life where you need healing? If so, one of the best places to start is to write him a letter. It may sound odd when you could just sit and talk to him about it, but we tend to be more specific and detailed when we write things down. As he did with Bartimaeus, he will ask you what you'd like him to do for you, so why don't you spend some time writing down your thoughts and feelings, and formulating your answer to that all-important question?

Talking it

- What's your favourite healing story in the Bible and why?
- What would you say most disrupts your relationship with God?
- Bartimaeus and the woman with menstrual problems were considered untouchable in their society. Is there anyone our society rejects and isolates in the same way?

Sustaining it

1 Journalling

One of the best ways to track your inner-healing journey is to keep a journal. Try to write in it regularly, recording your experiences and insights as you bring the deepest parts of yourself to God in prayer. It will help you see more clearly what is happening in you, and it will give you an amazing chronicle of God's healing power.

2 Worship in the waiting

Inner healing is rarely instant, so you can expect it to feel like a long journey. While you're walking that journey, it is crucial to keep your gaze fixed on the healer rather than the problems. Worship lifts our eyes from ourselves to Jesus, and it's surprising how much healing happens in us when we're not looking.

3 Don't go it alone

Bartimaeus and the woman had little choice about whether or not other people saw their healing, but we usually do, and it is tempting to keep the process to ourselves, for fear others might be embarrassed or judgemental. You don't need a crowd of hundreds, but it can be helpful to have a couple of people who know what you're journeying through. Why not tell a friend about the healing God is doing in you at the moment and ask them to support you in prayer?

Forgiveness
Matthew 6:14–15; Luke 15:11–32

Sidney felt terrible. He hadn't meant to smash his mum's favourite vase, but his set-piece goal had gone a bit wrong, and the football (which was banned from inside the house) had done the very thing his mum always said it would do. She was due home in five minutes, and there was no way Sidney had the nerve to face her and explain why he'd felt the need to practise his footwork in the lounge, so he swept all the pieces up and hid them under his bed.

It took a few days, but eventually Sidney's mum asked him, 'Sid, do you know where my vase is, the one that's normally on the mantelpiece?'

Sid stared at the floor. It was all a bit too much. He couldn't seem to stop thinking about the broken bits of vase, and he hadn't been able to look his mum in the eye since it had happened.

'I broke it,' he whispered.

'I know,' said his mum, putting a hand on his shoulder.

'How do you know? And if you knew, why did you ask about it?'

'I know because I'm the one who cleans your room and I found the pieces. And I didn't ask about it, because I wanted you to tell me. It's been bugging me. I hate there being this atmosphere between us. I forgave you as soon as I knew what you'd done, but I kind of hoped you'd feel you could talk to me about it.'

I have no idea where that story comes from, but it's been a favourite of mine since I was young. I love it because it sums up forgiveness so beautifully. That you and I will get things wrong is an inevitability; that we will do things that sadden God's heart is a certainty; but it is also a certainty that God's love for us does not change. Forgiveness is nothing more nor less than us, his flawed and fallible children, owning up to the things we've broken and asking his pardon, so that the relationship between us and him can spring to life again.

It's not a coincidence that Jesus' teaching on forgiveness often came hard on the heels of his teaching about prayer (Matthew 6:5–15, for instance). Prayer is relationship with God, so it will always show up anything that has ruptured or clogged up that relationship. If, like Sidney, you've ever tried to spend any time in the company of someone you need to forgive or confess to, you'll know how awkward that can be. If you want to grow or deepen your prayer life, then you're going to have to go on a journey of giving and receiving forgiveness.

Forgiveness starts with a journey back. The lost son in Jesus' parable was wasting away in a foreign land, but the moment he understood that he could ask for forgiveness, he was ready to start the journey home (Luke 15:11–20). Have you been reticent to pray lately because you know that, once you get 'home' to the Father's presence, you'll need to put something right with him? If that's what's keeping you, then don't waste another moment. Put the book down and spend some time with him. Life's too short to be alienated from the one who loves you completely, no matter what you've done.

Forgiveness needs to be asked for. Confession has been a part of prayer liturgy for centuries, because we human beings so often need to clear the ground of sin and selfishness before we can communicate freely with God. As Sidney so rightly observed, it can feel like a pointless thing to do – why do we tell God what we've done wrong when he already knows? – but as Sidney's mum knew, confession is what restores the warmth and intimacy in our relationship with God. Had the prodigal son gone home and tried to rebuild his relationship with his father without asking for forgiveness, it would have been a different story Jesus was telling. His father would likely still have received him, because he loved him and had already forgiven him, but there would have been awkwardness instead of closeness between them. Is there strain in your relationship with God because you're trying to hide, ignore or avoid something that you both know is tucked away under your metaphorical bed?

Forgiveness needs to be given. Perhaps the saddest part of Jesus' story of the lost son is the rupture in the father's relationship with the elder son. That rupture happened because the elder son wouldn't forgive his brother (Luke 15:25–32). In the end, that family was damaged more by unforgiveness than sin. That is a sobering thought.

Unforgiveness will always affect prayer. Jesus taught that God only forgives us when we forgive others (Matthew 6:14–15), so when we turn to God in prayer, we can't just hide our grudges behind our backs and ignore them until we're done. If our own hands are full of things we refuse to let go of, how can God give to us? If our hearts are brooding on the wrongs others have done to us, how can we have the conversations we need to have with him about our own flaws? If we have closed down in bitterness, how can he pour his endless grace into our lives?

Jesus' words sound scarily final, don't they? But be reassured: forgiveness is a slow and complex process, particularly when we have been severely wronged by others. God knows your wounds, and he doesn't want you to rush through the process of forgiving those who caused them. If all you can say at the moment is that you'd like to be able to forgive, even though you don't know where to start, that is enough for him. The elder son was bitter and in pain, and the father understood. He didn't force him to attend the party or condemn him for being unable to forgive. He simply reminded him of the unchanging truth that he was loved and included in the family, and that all the wealth of the household was available to him. If you can't forgive, God's love for you doesn't change, and his endless supply of grace and healing is always there for the asking.

Forgiveness needs to be received. The lost son came home ready to bunk down in the servants' quarters and live a life of drudgery because he didn't expect to be forgiven. In the story Jesus told, he received his father's forgiveness (Luke 15:20–24), but Jesus could equally have told a story of a young man being unable to accept what the father wanted to give, and choosing to live the life of a servant because that's all he thought he deserved. He would have lived in the same household as his father, but their every interaction would have been tinged with his sense of guilt and inadequacy.

When you pray, do you come boldly into God's presence, confident that the one who waits for you there is pleased to see you and delighted by your company, or do you creep in tentatively, feeling ashamed and inadequate? If the latter, then it's worth asking yourself whether you've refused his forgiveness at some point. Chances are you didn't do it deliberately; it usually happens by accident when we repent of something but then don't believe we deserve to be forgiven, so we keep wearing the shame like a servant's robe to remind ourselves that we should be doing better.

The father would not let the son wear a servant's robe. Instead, he gave him the robe of honour, the one worn by the most honoured and respected person in the household (Luke 15:22). Just to make sure he really knew he was forgiven, he also got shoes (servants didn't get to wear shoes) and the signet ring, the one used to seal business deals for the family. He'd squandered their fortune, but his father effectively handed him the family credit card. That's how complete the forgiveness was.

Do you need to throw off the servant's robe of guilt and inadequacy? Whatever you think of yourself, God has called you his child, and that is who you are. Knowing you are forgiven is a cue for celebration. Sidney and his mum probably went for chips, and the lost son got to be guest of honour at the biggest party the community had seen for a while. (You had to invite at least a hundred people if you didn't want to waste a fattened calf.)

I think it's safe to say that the younger son's relationship with his father ended up being better than it had ever been; not just better than it was during his rebellious years in a far-off land, but better than it had been even before that. Wounds and wrongs, whether ours or other people's, are painful things to work through, but it is typical of God's grace that, if we trust him to take us through those dark places in prayer, our relationship with him will be fuller, freer and more vibrant than it has ever been.

Trying it

Read the story of the lost son (Luke 15:11–32). Who do you associate with most in the story? Do you feel like the homecoming son, in need of forgiveness? Do you feel like the elder son, unable to forgive someone who has wronged you? Or do you feel like the bewildered honoured guest, struggling to accept your right to wear the family finery? Whoever it is, come to God in prayer. Ask him to show you what small step you can take towards giving or receiving forgiveness today, and then ask him to help you take it.

Talking it

- Have you ever been given something good that you thought you didn't deserve? How did it make you feel?
- What's the most helpful piece of advice you've ever heard about forgiveness?
- Have you ever seen God bring breakthrough in a situation of intractable conflict or relationship breakdown?

Sustaining it

1 Use pre-written prayers
The church has been using prayers of confession for centuries, and many of them can be found online. Why not find one and download it or print it so that you can use it regularly in your prayer rhythm?

2 Ask for grace
When forgiveness feels impossible, it's like a blocked drain. We can't shift the blockage, and the dirty water of resentment and bitterness backs up in us. Even if you can't clear the drain at the moment, you can ask God to pour grace into the mix every day. You won't feel much at first, but it will slowly work its way in, loosening the blockage and making forgiveness possible.

3 Celebrate restoration

Sometimes the best way to make something real is to celebrate it. If you've been struggling to believe you're forgiven – if you need help to choose the robe of honour instead of the cloak of guilt – why not do something to celebrate forgiveness? Treat yourself. Better still, tell someone else why you're celebrating, and treat them too.

Group prayer activity

Inner healing and forgiveness aren't easy to talk about in a group, but hand-washing is a good prayer action to use when talking isn't appropriate. Pass round a bowl of warm water, some soap and a towel, and invite each person to wash their hands, as a prayer for God to bring healing and restoration.

9

Voice and body

There is no power like that of prevailing prayer, of Abraham pleading for Sodom, Jacob wrestling in the stillness of the night, Moses standing in the breach, Hannah intoxicated with sorrow, David heartbroken with remorse and grief, Jesus in sweat of blood. Add to this list from the records of the church your personal observation and experience, and always there is the cost of passion unto blood. Such prayer prevails. It turns ordinary mortals into men of power. It brings power. It brings fire. It brings rain. It brings life. It brings God.

Samuel Chadwick, *The Complete Works of Samuel Chadwick* (CrossReach, 2016)

Praying with your body
Daniel 1:1–21; 3:1–30; 6:1–23

We have a Healing on the Streets ministry in the city where I live, and when we first launched it, I knew my work schedule wouldn't allow me to take part much, but I believed so passionately in what it was all about that I went along to the training. We spent the morning in a local church building, and then in the afternoon we ventured forth into the high street to put out our chairs, put up our 'Healing' banner and see who God might bring to us for prayer. Before any of that happened, though, we were invited to kneel on the pavement to spend a few minutes in silent prayer. Yes, I confess I did wonder why the praying wouldn't have been just as good standing up, but no sooner had my knees hit the ground than I knew what we were doing.

This wasn't a spoken prayer; it wasn't even just a silent prayer. This was a body prayer, and it was remarkably moving. As I knelt on the paving stones, my legs going numb and my mind whirring frantically over whether anyone I knew might be walking past at that precise moment, I understood why this mattered. It was us welcoming God's presence, not just with our minds and our words, but with our bodies. Kneeling was a physical demonstration of our willingness to humble ourselves. Kneeling in public was a demonstration of our willingness to lay down our pride and our need to look good. Kneeling in public in silence, amid a bustling city centre, was our bold, uncompromising statement that his presence and his work were more important than anything else that could happen in that place that afternoon. And as we held that sacred moment, the street where we knelt became a thin place.

Throughout the Bible, we find people using their bodies to pray. Whether it's lying prostrate in worship, sitting on the floor in sackcloth and ashes, kneeling in supplication or standing up ready for action, people have used body posture in prayer to accentuate their words. It's not surprising, since we use our bodies in all kinds of communication. Try talking excitedly about something without leaning forwards. Try complimenting someone without smiling. Our bodies naturally mirror and emphasise what we say with our words, so why not in prayer?

If you've ever read the book of Daniel, you'll know he was a man who prayed, but have you ever noticed the part body posture had to play in his story?

He and his three friends were promising young leaders in Jerusalem when the kingdom of Judah was attacked by the Babylonians. Babylon's strategy was to take the brightest and best from each of the nations they conquered, and to gather them at Nebuchadnezzar's court for training in Babylonian culture, with a view to appointing them as leaders across the empire. Right from day one in their new life, Daniel, Hananiah, Mishael and Azariah (who were renamed

Belteshazzar, Shadrach, Meshach and Abednego) were left in no doubt that their minds needed to be in peak condition, but so did their bodies. They were Nebuchadnezzar's elite, and they needed to embody his brand at all times.

But these four young men had been brought up to know that what you do with your body is just as powerful and important as what you do with your mind, and they weren't about to let their bodies be adverts for anything they didn't believe in. Instead they used their bodies in worship and prayer to the God of Israel, right in the middle of that pagan court. It got them into all sorts of very physical trouble – not least a lion's den and a fiery furnace – but it also opened thin places where God could touch many lives.

Perhaps the most familiar prayer posture is kneeling, and it's the one that got Daniel booked in for a night with the aforementioned lions (Daniel 6:1–23). It all started with a decree telling everyone they had to worship the king. Daniel was an old man by this time, and it was by no means the first time this kind of decree had been issued. He could probably have found discreet ways around it – worshipping God without drawing attention to himself – yet he made an obvious point of going to his room three times a day, facing Jerusalem and kneeling in prayer. And it was almost certainly the kneeling that sealed his fate when the officials came to check what he was up to. Had he been sitting or standing, he could probably have hidden the fact that he was praying, but kneeling was unmistakable proof of prayer, and kneeling towards Jerusalem was unmistakable proof of prayer to the God of Israel.

By this stage in his life, Daniel was a highly respected leader in Babylon, and it would have made sense for him not to do anything to jeopardise that, but he had a different story to tell. He knew that he owed everything to the God of Israel, the God he had served all his life. No matter how much wealth and power the Babylonian empire could give him, his prime allegiance was to God alone. Kneeling was an act of submission and a prayer of trust.

There was another occasion when I found myself kneeling on a pavement. We were outside Canterbury's guildhall, the place that for centuries has represented ultimate human power in the city, and we wanted to pray for God's kingdom to come and for his will to be done here. We could have prayed all those things in an unobtrusive (and far more comfortable) way, but the prayer didn't feel complete until we had used our bodies to express it. The kneeling didn't make the prayer more powerful, but it did help us to connect more deeply with the words we were saying.

Not only is kneeling a posture of humility and surrender, but it's also one of the most uncomfortable postures you can hold for any length of time if you're not used to it. Discomfort focuses the mind. It's hard for your thoughts to drift when you're working hard to hold an uncomfortable position, so kneeling comes into its own when you want to pray for something in a focused way.

If the body posture of kneeling emphasises humility and trust, then standing emphasises determination and a readiness to fight. When Daniel and his friends were still relatively young, Nebuchadnezzar proclaimed himself a god and issued a decree that at the sound of the imperial orchestra everyone should prostrate themselves. Shadrach, Meshach and Abednego refused. They knew that to prostrate one's body was an act of worship, and they had no intention of worshipping anyone except the God of Israel, even if it cost them their lives. They remained upright as a sign of resistance, and it got them thrown into a furnace (Daniel 3:1–30). Their standing was as much a prayer as Daniel's kneeling. It was a defiant vigil, calling for God's power to break through in that terrifying cacophony of mass brainwashing.

Many people find that prayer comes alive for them when they can use their bodies as well as their words. It's wonderful to be able to tell God that we adore him, but it takes that wonder to a new level if you can dance before him in adoration. It's powerful to pray for someone, but it's often even more powerful if you can lay a hand on their shoulder as you pray. Telling God you surrender to him is a profound moment in prayer, but you may find it resonates even more if you lie face down as you say it. And even if those ideas sound too ambitious, you can do something as simple as holding your hands in different positions as you pray, to embody what you're saying to God: turn your hands palms down as you ask him to help you let go of your burdens and cares, then turn them palms up as you invite him to fill you with love and patience, for instance.

Daniel and his friends had one other way of embodying their prayers, and that was through fasting. In those first months of exile in Babylon, they needed to find ways of worshipping Yahweh even while they were being trained by Nebuchadnezzar's court. Perhaps they were too young and nervous to do the courageous things they did later in life, but they knew they needed to do something to avoid offending God by eating food that was unclean, so they requested a simpler diet (Daniel 1:1–21). They didn't say why they were abstaining, and the officials possibly thought it was a self-imposed endurance test, but in fact it was an act of worship and an embodied prayer. Their abstinence was an affirmation of their faith in God and a cry for his help in that distant, alien land. God's answer was swift and complete. They didn't just survive, they thrived; they weren't just tolerated, they found favour; they didn't just maintain their own faith, they saw thousands of Babylonians come to faith in Yahweh – even the rulers themselves.

Learning to fast definitely hasn't been my favourite prayer discipline, and it isn't possible for everyone, but I have found it to be a powerful way of embodying my prayers. When I feel the pangs of hunger, I immediately ask myself which I want more – physical food or the things I'm fasting for. That way, even the hunger pangs become like prayers rumbling around in my stomach. Of course, fasting doesn't have to mean stopping eating altogether. You may choose to fast from particular foods (like Daniel and his friends did), or from social media or television, for instance. Whatever it is, the principle is the same. We deny ourselves something we would normally enjoy or rely on, and that denial becomes a prayer. As we hunger for whatever we've given up, we're making our wordless declaration that we long for God more than anything else in this world.

Trying it

Pray your way through Psalm 51, using different body postures to accentuate the words you're saying. This exercise might be easier if you listen to the words being read, rather than reading them yourself. You could either use the audio playback in your Bible app, or make a recording of yourself reading the psalm slowly and then play it back.

- Lie face down on the floor and read verses 1–6. This is a posture of worship and penitence.
- Kneel to read verses 7–14. This is a posture of humility and supplication.
- Stand to read verses 15–19. This is a posture of declaration and determination.

Talking it

- Have you ever chosen to use a particular posture while you've been praying? Why did you choose it, and how did it change the way you prayed?
- Do you think it matters whether or not Christians fast?
- When you gather for worship as a church, which prayer postures do you tend to use most often? Are there others you could invite people to use?

Sustaining it

1 Make space for movement
If you don't usually have much space or privacy when you pray, then body posture and movement can be difficult to include in your prayer rhythm. Praying on the train on your commute to work may be a good use of time, but it probably doesn't lend itself to kneeling

or lying prostrate on the floor! Try to make times and spaces where your prayer can become more physical.

2 Try it in company
If you're praying with others and you feel comfortable, why not change your posture to accentuate your prayers? You could kneel during sung worship in church, or stand up to emphasise a prayer you're praying in your small group, perhaps. Movement or posture shift can help bring corporate prayer to life.

3 Learn more about fasting
We've touched briefly on fasting in this chapter, but it can become a precious part of your prayer rhythm. Why not read more about it, and ask God to show you how, when and where you could practise it?

Praying out loud
1 Samuel 1:12–17; 1 Kings 17:1; 18:41–45; Psalm 28:7; James 5:17–18; 1 Corinthians 14:13–19

The family were dressed in their best, the house was looking cleaner than it had for months, and mum and dad were only slightly stressed. They'd all been dreading this dinner for weeks, but now the guests were here and it was time to sit down at the table. Ellie thought she would be the one who had to say grace, and she'd been planning her best prayer for days, so she was really shocked when her dad asked her little brother Josh to do it. Josh was shocked too, by all accounts, since he just stared back at his dad in dumb horror. After quite a lot of awkward silence, Dad did one of his really big, stressy sighs and said, 'Just say the prayer I said at breakfast this morning, Josh.'

Looking a little doubtful, Josh took a deep breath and opened his mouth: 'Dear God, thank you for this food… and help us all have a great day, even though we've got those annoying people coming for dinner.'

Praying out loud has a habit of exposing us, as ably demonstrated by Josh and his dad that day. It is something that many, many people find very difficult, yet it is well worth exploring. The fact that we need to explore it at all is largely a product of our times. The Bible is full of examples of people praying out loud, both in private and in corporate prayer, because religion was something that families and communities practised together. Nowadays, faith is often the preserve of the individual. We may go to church, but chances are our daily rhythms of prayer are practised almost entirely in private. We might conclude that praying out loud matters less if we don't need to express ourselves for the benefit of others, but that would be to miss out on a rich and beautiful facet of personal prayer.

Delving into scripture, we discover that there are several reasons why people spoke out loud in prayer. Sometimes, of course, it was to lead and inspire others; often it was a kind of overflow. The psalms are full of people who found their joy bursting out of them in spoken words and songs.

> You are my strength and my shield from every danger. When I fully trust in you, help is on the way. I jump for joy and burst forth with ecstatic, passionate praise!
> PSALM 28:7 (TPT)

Yet the overflow could just as easily be out of desperation. Hannah had been unable to get pregnant, so she went into the place of worship at Shiloh to pray. As she wept and poured out her heart, her prayers spilled out in spoken words (1 Samuel 1:12–17). She clearly didn't mean them to be heard, since she kept her voice to a whisper, but neither could she keep them in. Do you ever find your emotions so stirred in prayer that you simply have to say something – or sing something? If so, then you're experiencing that overflow.

On other occasions, the speaking out was more of a command from God. You're probably familiar with the Old Testament prophets and their role of bringing God's word into different situations, but did you know that there appears to be a crossover between prophetic utterance and prayer? It's as though, by speaking out what they'd heard from God, they were also somehow praying it into being.

Elijah was given the daunting task of starting and ending a drought. In the account in 1 Kings (17:1; 18:41–45), we read that he spoke the drought into being, and then declared it to be at an end a few years later. Yet the apostle James puts a slightly different slant on it:

> Elijah was a human being, even as we are. He prayed earnestly that it would not rain, and it did not rain on the land for three and a half years. Again he prayed, and the heavens gave rain, and the earth produced its crops.
> JAMES 5:17–18

Did Elijah declare it or did he pray it? Or is there a link between the two? I've certainly known times when I've felt a strong nudge to speak something out loud, knowing that it falls somewhere in that crossover between prayer and prophecy. It often happens when I'm praying for the city where I live, for instance. I get a thought or a word from God and it's prophetic. That doesn't necessarily mean it's predicting the future; it usually means it's something he is saying he wants to do here, if only we will welcome his Spirit's working. And I know I need to speak it out loud. It's not that my speaking it has any magic power to make it happen – only God can do that – but neither can I simply hold it in my heart as a silent prayer. It needs to be spoken out as a prayerful prophecy, or a prophetic prayer. Had Elijah not spoken, a reign of tyranny might have gone on far longer than it did. Who knows what our prophetic prayers might unleash in our communities?

As if these weren't good enough reasons to pray out loud, the whole landscape of prayer got a radical addition on the day of Pentecost. The Holy Spirit came, and among his many gifts was the ability to speak in different languages. Initially this gift was used primarily for evangelism – thousands of people heard the gospel in their own language that day – but it was clearly also given as a way of praying. By the time Paul wrote his letter to the church in Corinth, he was teaching it as a component of prayer (1 Corinthians 14:1–19). He didn't think it was essential that they be able to pray in tongues – in fact, he was concerned that they were putting too much emphasis on it – but he saw it as a valuable part of his own prayer life.

> For if I am praying in a tongue, my spirit is engaged in prayer but I have no clear understanding of what is being said. So here's what I've concluded. I will pray in the Spirit, but I will also pray with my mind engaged. I will sing rapturous praises in the Spirit, but I will also sing with my mind engaged.
>
> 1 CORINTHIANS 14:14–15 (TPT)

I find that my intellect is prone to get in the way when I pray. Its contributions are usually welcome, but sometimes I know I need to step beyond logical, rational thinking. I need to let the Spirit lead me without my intellect popping up like an aggrieved satnav, telling me to make a U-turn where possible. To pray in tongues is to let the Spirit pray through us, using our voices to pray his prayers. It certainly shouldn't be the only kind of praying we do (our intellects are as much a gift from God as his Spirit is), but it enriches prayer in remarkable ways.

Trying it

God loves to hear your voice, even if you find it rather uncomfortable to listen to. Next time you pray, find a place where no one can hear you and do all your praying out loud. Try not to get hung up on the words you're saying; just speak. Get used to the sound of your own voice in prayer.

Talking it

- Have you found it difficult to pray out loud in the past, either on your own or in a group? Why do you think that is?

- Do you know of a situation where someone has spoken out a prophetic prayer and things have changed?
- Do you have the gift of tongues? When and how did you receive it?

Sustaining it

1 Pray in tongues regularly
Many of us get used to using the gift of tongues in corporate worship, but forget about it when it comes to personal prayer. It is an excellent discipline to put your own agenda aside for a while and simply let the Spirit pray through you. As you form the words he's giving you, listen with your own spirit and see if you get any sense of what you're praying. It doesn't matter if you don't, but you might be surprised to find you can sense where he is leading you.

2 Sing the psalms
The psalms are songs. They were written to be sung, not read aloud, so why not sing them? It doesn't matter whether you think you can sing or not. God loves your voice, so just choose a psalm and start singing the words. You could use a tune you already know or make one up.

3 Practise prophetic prayer
It's unlikely that God is asking you to speak a drought into being, like Elijah did, but he may have given you a word of encouragement for a situation you've been praying about. Don't just hold it in your heart; speak it out: pray it out loud and tell others about it. As you speak it, it becomes a prophetic prayer that begins to impact the situation you're praying for.

Group prayer activity

Choose a psalm and invite the group to read it aloud – not all together, but each person taking it in turns to read a verse. Encourage people to notice and enjoy the diversity of each other's voices.

10

Scripture

Men and women are needed whose prayers will give to the world the utmost power of God; who will make His promises to blossom with rich and full results. God is waiting to hear us and challenges us to bring Him to do this thing by our praying.

E.M. Bounds, *The Weapon of Prayer* (Destiny Image, 1978)

Power and promise
Psalm 119:105–120; Hebrews 4:12; 1 Peter 1:23

The Bible has now been translated into over 3,300 languages. That's an impressive feat, but it pales a little when you realise that there are still 1.5 billion people in the world who don't have access to the full scriptures in their own language – or their 'heart language', as translators call it. There are still almost 2,000 languages into which no one has even started translating the Bible yet.

I remember once reading the story of a community in a remote rural location which was visited by missionaries. As people began to come to faith, they were keen to have a copy of the Bible, but the missionaries had only one copy available to them, so they decided to divide it up, leaving a few pages with each village they visited. The village I was reading about had been left a few chapters of Jeremiah – and not the cheerful chapters at that – yet those flimsy pages became the most precious thing the community owned.

Whether you're reading the joyful bits or the more depressing bits, God's word has power, and every single bit of it is worth absorbing.

Psalm 119 is a glorious celebration of the word of God. It was written many centuries before the formation of the Bible as we know it, but God's people had long since begun to write down his laws and statutes, learning them by heart, living them out and teaching them to their children. It's the longest psalm in the Bible and it's full of wisdom, but we'll focus in on just three points, because they help us understand the way prayer and scripture bring each other to life.

> Your word is a lamp for my feet, a light on my path.
> PSALM 119:105

If you've ever met someone with a torch on a dark night, you'll know that light can be both useful and unhelpful, depending on the circumstances. If your eyes are used to the dark and someone suddenly waves a light in front of your face, it's completely useless to you because it blinds you. You can only make use of light when your eyes have adjusted to it. I've had times in my life when I've done the same thing with the word of God. A situation has been troubling me, so I've opened the Bible in the hope of discovering the perfect solution, only to find myself more confused than ever. That's because I was trying to look into the light of scripture without the habit of prayer.

God's word is always a light, but it's prayer that enables our eyes to adjust so that we can see by it. That's because prayer is where we get to know God himself. Only when we begin to know him can we possibly understand what he meant when he inspired the men and women who wrote down his ways and precepts in the scriptures. We can probably all think of situations where verses from the Bible have been wrenched out of context and used in such a way that they do far more harm than good. The reason we cringe when seeing that happening is because we know that the words have somehow been used in a way that contradicts the character of the God who inspired them. His word can only light your way if you learn to walk with him, holding the lamp in one hand and putting your other hand in his.

The other reason prayer is so crucial in helping us make the best use of that precious lamp is that no light is any good at all if we just stare into it. Light sources exist to illuminate something else. In this case, the psalmist says that the light of the word illuminates our feet on the path of our lives. Were you to open your Bible now and read a verse or two, you might well find the words encouraging, but only if you then take time to hold them for a while in prayer will you really see how they apply to your life. It's when you pray that you allow God to direct the beam of the lamp so that it shows what he wants you to see.

> I'm bruised and broken, overwhelmed by it all; breathe life into
> me again by your living word.
> PSALM 119:107 (TPT)

The word of God isn't a reference book. Of course, it's very handy to have it in book form, but it's not a set of instructions to live by or an encyclopedia for life – though we may well find all kinds of advice in it. It's something living and active. The writer to the Hebrews described it as 'full of power [making it operative, energising and effective]' (Hebrews 4:12, AMP). It isn't merely a repository of useful information; it changes things. Later in the Hebrews verse, the writer describes it as a double-edged sword. That implies it's something that you wield, rather than something you just absorb, and it's this wielding that involves prayer. We don't wield the sword of God's word by simply speaking it out loud. That would make it a magic spell, and it definitely isn't that. We wield it by loving it, knowing its author, understanding its meaning and then praying it into the situations where it is needed.

Do you ever come across words of comfort and strength in scripture and find yourself wishing they were your lived experience, particularly in those times when you feel broken and overwhelmed?

Prayer is the act by which you apply the power of those words to your life. Do you ever come across words that seem perfect for someone else's situation? You might opt to share those words with them, but do you also pray those words for them? Do you take time to wield the sword and pray blessing over their lives?

> You are my refuge and my shield; I have put my hope in your word… Sustain me, my God, according to your promise, and I shall live; do not let my hopes be dashed.
>
> PSALM 119:114, 116

The word of God isn't a history book. It tells tales of the past, and even the newest parts of it are already almost 2,000 years old, but it has no use-by date on it. It is as true and powerful today as it has ever been. If you read it and find words that seem as though they were written for you, it's because they were. The word of God has layers and layers of meaning, making it still relevant today, and the one who inspired it, from the timeless furnace of his heart, already had you in mind long before he began imparting it to men and women to write down.

The apostle Peter likens the word of God to imperishable seed that is planted in us and keeps producing new life (1 Peter 1:23). When a phrase from that living word jumps off the page at you and seems to land deep in the soil of your heart, it's because it's a truth God wants to grow in you, and a promise that is meant to keep sustaining you, no matter where life takes you. The trouble is, I don't know about you, but I'm about as good with those seeds as I am with house plants: I have a gift for forgetting about them, and then wondering why they die on me. When a seed of promise gets planted in us, we need to keep nurturing it: we need to remind ourselves of it, to pray it over ourselves, to hold on to it by faith and to trust its author to fulfil it in his way and in his time.

Trying it

Next time you're stopping to pray, try savouring a few words from God's eternal, active word. For instance, savour the phrase 'The Lord is my rock'. Say it to yourself several times over, each time putting the emphasis on a different word in the phrase: '*The* Lord is my rock'; 'The *Lord* is my rock'; 'The Lord *is* my rock'; and so on. Stop after each phrase and reflect on how emphasising a different word gives the whole phrase fresh nuance. Then ask God which version of the phrase he is emphasising to you at this time in your life.

Talking it

- Have you ever known a phrase or story from the Bible to change your life in a powerful way? Which phrase or story was it, and how did it happen?
- Is there a promise that God has planted in you like seed? What has he promised, and how do you make sure you keep hold of it and keep nurturing it?
- When we gather for worship together, our church services usually involve a reading from the Bible. Are there things we could do to help remind each other that the Bible isn't just a book; it's active, powerful and alive?

Sustaining it

1 Read every day
No matter what your prayer rhythm is like, and no matter how busy you are, it is a good idea to drink in some words of scripture every day. Whether it's subscribing to daily Bible reading notes, checking the 'verse of the day' on your Bible app or working your way through a particular book of the Bible by reading a few verses each day, find a way of dipping into scripture as part of your daily routine.

2 Read and stop
Get into the habit of stopping to pray, even for a minute or two,

after you read scripture. Give God space to angle the lamp, so that it shines where he wants it to in your life. Try not to rush on, assuming you know what the verses you read mean. Give him time to show you other layers of meaning that you may not previously have noticed.

3 Read and wield

When you come across a situation that needs to change, whether in your own life or someone else's, develop the habit of asking God to show you a word or phrase in scripture that you can wield in prayer. Then, each time you are prompted to pray for that situation, don't just ask God for his help; take the word or phrase he's given you and shape your prayer around it. For instance, you might be praying for more strength because you feel tired, and God might draw your attention to the words in Isaiah that talk about him giving strength to the weary and increasing the power of the weak (Isaiah 40:29). Instead of simply asking him to help you in your tiredness, your prayer becomes a declaration of truth and faith: 'Lord, thank you that you have strength to give me, and that you can increase the power in me even when I feel weak. Help me draw all I need from you today. Amen.'

Justice and kingdom
2 Kings 22:1—23:25

In 2016, I became the moderator for the Christians Together group in our city. My term lasted one year, and just as it began, I received several emails about an issue that seemed to be gaining traction in our local press. A London borough had purchased houses on the outskirts of our city, to accommodate some 200 families for whom they couldn't find homes within their district. There was a degree of understandable frustration from local groups, because our own council had a housing shortage, but the Christians Together committee became concerned when coverage of the issue in the local press took a distinctly vitriolic and racist turn. There seemed to be a campaign to stir people up against this planned resettlement.

Not being sure what else to do, we decided to call a meeting, gathering representatives from churches, charities, residents' groups and the two borough councils in question. We had only expected about 20 people, but the hall was packed. This was clearly an issue that people felt strongly about.

I have lived here for over 25 years, but that evening will go down as one of my proudest moments in this city. I was chairing the meeting, and I listened as church representative after church representative took the microphone and declared to everyone present that we as the church would not sit by and see newcomers to our city treated with disrespect or racism, because God requires his people to be generous, hospitable and open-hearted. They may not have been quoting Bible verses verbatim, but they were all speaking out scriptural principles. No matter what the needs of our own community might be, we would welcome the families from the London borough with open arms, because that is what God's word teaches us to do for those in need.

By the end of the meeting, we had agreed to work together as churches to pack a welcome bag for each new family as a way of helping them to feel at home in our city.

It is the job of God's people to live out the precepts and principles of God's word in such a way that our villages, towns and cities are transformed into kinder, fairer places that look more and more like God's kingdom. King Josiah took that responsibility very seriously indeed. When he was only a young man, he ordered some renovations to be made to the temple and, during the works, a book of the law was found (2 Kings 22:1–10). It probably wasn't the whole law of Moses, but a part that somehow had been overlooked and which, Josiah realised, the people hadn't been obeying for many, many years. He was distraught, and went to work putting things right.

The first thing he did was to make sure the people knew what the forgotten book said (2 Kings 23:1–2). God's people have a responsibility to publish his word to our communities, because it is life-giving and life-transforming. In Josiah's case it was a full reading of the forgotten book; in the case of our public meeting, it was church members articulating the values of God's word in their responses to the resettlement project. Yet, as we learnt in the first section of this chapter, we can't just shout it out and hope for the best. We need to pray it in; otherwise it can't do its work. As soon as the reading of the lost book had finished, Josiah led the people in a prayer of covenant (2 Kings 23:3). Many centuries later, we too finished our public meeting with a prayer of commitment that we would hold fast to the principles of generosity and kindness towards each of the 200 families moving to our city. As we put our welcome-bag plan into action, there was certainly a lot of prayer going on. Powerful though a simple gift can be, we wanted those bags to do something more. We wanted them to communicate the love and generosity we read about in the Bible.

Some weeks after the families began arriving, I talked to one of the ladies who had received a bag on her first day in her new home. She said that what had touched her most wasn't the teabags or the lightbulbs, but the kindness with which the bag had been given. I was thrilled! She hadn't just got the bag, but she'd got the message too – the message that she is loved and welcome. The word of God had reached her because of our prayers.

The second thing Josiah did was to act on the words he had read. He didn't just preach them as a judgement; he also demonstrated them by the way he lived. He instigated a thorough clean-up of the temple and the nation, because neither place looked anything like the kind of community that the forgotten book described (2 Kings 23:4–20). The church has a sad history of preaching without living. We have told people what they're doing wrong – lacing Bible verses through our sermons like vicious barbs – yet we have often failed to demonstrate what a society founded on godly principles would look like, and we have failed to work to make it a reality. It is wonderful to preach the word of God. It is wonderful to pray it in, so that it becomes a living and active influence in our communities. But we need to make sure that some of that prayer is expressed in action – getting our hands dirty in the business of kingdom-building. God needs people who will embody his word, as well as preaching it and praying it.

Josiah had been devoted to God from an early age, but reading that lost book of the law ignited something new in him. He could suddenly see the insidious darkness that had slowly settled across the nation, and he knew he needed to deal with it. Much of what he did in his clean-up involved decommissioning sites of pagan worship. The spiritual atmosphere of the country had become dark and confused by all kinds of evil. He even had to dismantle a furnace commonly used for child sacrifice. Reading the book shed light on the darkness of his land, but praying it gave him the power and authority he needed to push back that darkness. He would certainly have faced opposition as he dismantled cults that had prospered for decades, but reading and praying God's word had released a power that swept the whole land clean.

The word of God is the searchlight that sweeps its beam into the darkest corners of our society, and bids us take a stand against every power that oppresses and enslaves. That standing is primarily a work of prayer. Just as prayer wields the sword of God's word to bring breakthrough in our own lives, so it does the same for our towns and cities. When God's people pray God's word in a place, darkness must retreat.

There is strong evidence to suggest that the book Josiah discovered was the book of Deuteronomy, since it is the section of the Torah that is most vehement about the worship of other gods and the practice of witchcraft, both of which had apparently been going on unhindered in Jerusalem for decades. Yet it also contains some wonderful descriptions of what a community can look like when it is shaped by God's principles and precepts.

All these blessings will come down on you and spread out beyond you because you have responded to the Voice of God, your God: God's blessing inside the city, God's blessing in the country; God's blessing on your children, the crops of your land, the young of your livestock, the calves of your herds, the lambs of your flocks. God's blessing on your basket and bread bowl; God's blessing in your coming in, God's blessing in your going out. God will defeat your enemies who attack you.

DEUTERONOMY 28:2–7 (MSG)

If we're going to pray the word of God for our communities, it's not enough to have a hatred of darkness. We need to have a vision of what the place we're praying for could look like. Then we can wield the sword of his word to overcome the work of the enemy, but we can also sow imperishable seeds of hope that will grow to a harvest of justice and peace.

Trying it

Read Deuteronomy 28:1–14 and see if you can write the same sort of blessing prayer for the place where you live. Moses' words were spoken to people living in an agrarian society, for whom crops and cattle were a major concern, but that may not be the case for your village, town or city. Open the eyes of your imagination and write down a list of the blessings you believe you would see springing up in your local community if it was wholly shaped by God's word and God's kingdom.

Talking it

- Do the churches where you live 'preach' God's word to the local community? Are there things happening that help people understand who God is and what he's like?
- Have you ever seen the Bible used to harm people instead of blessing them? How can we make sure we always use scripture in a way that mirrors God's character?

- Where do you see darkness and oppression at work in your local community? What would you most love to see changed?

Sustaining it

1 Sow a promise
Praying for your local community can be discouraging and hard going if you don't have a vision for how things could be. Change for change's sake is never enough to motivate us. We need to know where we're headed. Ask God to give you a phrase, verse or passage of scripture as a promise for the place where you live. Each time you're out and about, pray that promise, sowing it like an imperishable seed of hope wherever you go.

2 See beneath the surface
Seeing things for what they are can be difficult if you know a place well. It's easy to get so used to what's going on that you miss things. Make time to chat to someone who's relatively new to the area, and ask them what darkness and oppression they've noticed as they've got to know the place and its people.

3 Get involved
What do you long to see changed in your community? What is the seed of promise you're sowing daily through your prayers? What could you do to get involved in bringing about the change you long to see? As you pray and live out God's word, others will see it and want to know more.

Group prayer activity

Ask each member of the group to choose a promise from the Bible that they'd like to see come true in your local community. Print a sheet with all the promises on it, and read it out together as your 'scripture prayer' for the place where you live.

11

Warfare

There is a spiritual war in progress, an all-out moral battle. There is evil and cruelty, unhappiness and illness. There is superstition and ignorance, brutality and pain. God is in continuous and energetic battle against all of it. God is for life and against death. God is for love and against hate. God is for hope and against despair. God is for heaven and against hell. There is no neutral ground in the universe. Every square foot of space is contested.

Eugene H. Peterson, *Run with the Horses: The quest for life at its best* (IVP, 2008)

Opposition strategies
Genesis 3:1–5; Exodus 5:1—6:9; John 8:44; 10:10; Revelation 12:10–11

I once perforated my eyeball. Sorry if you're eating just now; I'll save you the gory details. I banged into something that hit me hard in the eye, and the rest, as they say, is medical history. The normal course of action after a trauma like that is for an ophthalmic surgeon to put gas or oil into the eye to prevent the retina from detaching, but since my eyes didn't form properly before I was born, no one knows what's in them, how they work (or don't work) or how you'd put them back together again if you had to dismantle them for any reason, so the consultant wasn't keen to do it. He warned me that a detachment was likely, but we were all hoping for the best, and a bunch of us were also praying.

Fast forward almost three months and it was looking good. I had been discharged from the hospital and there was no sign of a detachment. I then started working on some plans to hold a 24-7 prayer week in a shop in the centre of Canterbury. But on the day of the first planning meeting, as I stood on the train platform for my usual commute to work, I realised I had lost vision in the perforated eye. The detachment was happening.

This chapter is about spiritual warfare, so am I telling you this story because I believe that Satan, God's cosmic enemy, caused my retina to detach? No. I have no idea why it detached on that day. I'm telling you the story because it is my experience that when we get intentional about prayer, we almost always face opposition or pressure of some kind. For me, the run-up to that amazing city-centre prayer week will forever be associated with the stress of multiple trips to a London eye hospital and a groundbreaking medical procedure that applied the necessary silicon oil to stop my retina peeling off any further.

The Israelites were living in slavery, and Moses wanted to do something about it, so God instructed him to go to Pharaoh and ask him to let the slaves have three days off to worship at Mount Sinai. They needed to stop working, get away and reconnect with Yahweh. And yet, no sooner had the plan been put into action than all hell seemed to break loose (Exodus 5:1–21).

Does that sound familiar? Have you ever set out to pray, or to help others pray, only to find your way blocked by all sorts of random, frustrating things? It certainly isn't all Satan's fault; we are quite capable of getting distracted, being pulled in several different directions by the needs of others or just lacking the determination to do what we need to do. But the Bible is clear that there is an intelligent, intentional presence in our universe that opposes the work of God. Jesus called it 'Satan' or 'the devil', and he taught about it on several different occasions, so it's clearly something we need to understand. Indeed, it was this malign presence that Jesus met on his own journey to worship in the desert. The Bible is full of stories of God's people facing opposition for wanting to pray to and worship him, and this story from Exodus is one of them. I'm not suggesting that Pharaoh was Satan personified, but the story has some excellent lessons for us about the kinds of opposition we ourselves might face when we set our hearts and minds to prayer.

The first thing Pharaoh did in response to Moses' request was to make the Israelite slaves busier. He took away their supply of straw, but expected them still to make just as many bricks (Exodus 5:6–14). In 2014, I was producing a video prayer course for The Salvation Army, and we interviewed about 20 people at one of the Christian summer conferences, asking them what was most likely to stop them praying. The results were fascinating: every single adult gave either busyness or distraction as their answer.

Our lives don't get busy because the devil piles up things for us to do. The things that make us busy are usually good things that need doing. Yet that feeling of overwhelming pressure – the fear that we will be letting people down if we don't juggle all the balls, spin all the plates and meet all the deadlines – just might be an enemy tactic. Jesus described Satan as a thief who 'comes only to steal and kill and destroy' (John 10:10). If busyness is stealing from you, if it is killing your prayer life and destroying the balance of your days, then it is opposition and it needs dealing with. Later in this same verse, Jesus went on to say that he had come to give 'life in its fullness until you overflow' (TPT). If you're not overflowing with abundant life, if you've got less and less straw, but more and more bricks to make, then you're living under tyranny, and that's not what God ever intended for you.

It proved a bad move to try to reason with Pharaoh. The next thing the Israelites got was a barrage of accusations and insults about how lazy they were (Exodus 5:15–18). It's not at all unusual to press into prayer, only to find yourself harangued by self-doubt and false guilt. The name 'Satan' means 'adversary' or 'accuser'. In his vision on

Patmos, the apostle John heard him referred to as 'the accuser of our brothers and sisters' (Revelation 12:10). If you settle down to pray, only to find accusation and self-recrimination bubbling up, that is an enemy tactic. If the Holy Spirit needs to convict you of something you've done wrong, then he will be clear about exactly what it is he's referring to, and hope will surge in you, even as you confess and ask forgiveness. But if all you feel is a vague sense of guilt and failure, accompanied by a liberal dose of hopelessness, then you're under accusation, and that's not what God wants for you.

The next verse in Revelation goes on to say that the accuser has been overcome by 'the blood of the Lamb' (Revelation 12:11). In that beautiful way the Bible has of bringing stories full circle, this is a reminder of how the Israelites were eventually liberated through the Passover – the feast where the blood of a lamb was daubed over the doorway of each of their houses – and of the timeless truth that you and I are made righteous not by any efforts of our own to get things right, but by the lifeblood of the lamb of God, shed for us on a cross 2,000 years ago.

In our survey of what stops people praying, while adults were unanimous in saying it was busyness, young people had different answers. One young lad told me that the only time he found it hard to pray was when he felt angry with a friend of his. The Israelites found much the same thing. Their leaders came back from Pharaoh, battered by unreasonable demands and accusations, and the next thing that happened was that they fell out with their friends (Exodus 5:19–21). Moses and Aaron had come to help them, but they ended up arguing.

There are two kinds of discord. Sometimes we argue because we disagree with each other, and that's normal and healthy, but all too often we fall out with each other because we've started to believe lies about the other person. How often have you tried to pray about something – anything – only to find your mind constantly drawn back to a tension in a relationship? And how quickly do you hear yourself reciting all the unfair things the person might be thinking or saying about you, most of which are frankly pure speculation on your part? It won't surprise you, then, to know that Jesus called Satan a 'liar' and 'the father of lies' (John 8:44). Once you start believing lies about someone, your prayers for them become inaccurate and ineffective and are more likely to stem from frustration and indignation than from genuine love and compassion. Truth is all-important in prayer, and the enemy knows it.

Another young person who responded to our survey said that she was most likely to stop praying when she hadn't got the answer she wanted from God. Her very honest response neatly sums up what happened next in the Exodus story. Moses went back to God with a heart full of disappointment (Exodus 5:22–23). God had failed them. God had made unreasonable demands. God had not done his part. The first time we meet Satan in the Bible is in Genesis 3. He is depicted as a serpent, slithering into paradise to test the mettle of this beautiful new relationship between God and his people, and his tactic is to start questioning whether God was treating them fairly and whether he could be trusted at all (Genesis 3:1–5).

You've beaten the busyness; you've spotted and dispatched the accusation and the lies; and now you're faced with the agony of wondering why God hasn't answered your prayers. Each prayer time seems like a painful rehearsal of all the reasons why he has failed you, so you pray less and less. Arguing with God is no bad thing. He is more than robust enough to hear your grievances. Doubting his intentions and questioning his methods are also perfectly normal things to do in prayer. He is beyond our understanding and his ways are mysterious. But when disappointment takes hold, it can produce a pernicious suspicion deep within us that God doesn't really care about us, and that he doesn't really have our best interests at heart.

God's answer to his people comprised two key phrases: '*I am* the Lord', and '*I will* bring you out...' (Exodus 6:6). When the enemy sows doubt and disappointment, those phrases are always God's response. The great 'I am' has not changed, and we are not yet at the end of his story. The 'I will' is still to come.

Trying it

Next time you make space in your life for prayer, try to notice what derails you. Awareness is one of the most helpful tools when it comes to dealing with opposition. As you notice things, take your stand and ask for God's protection. You might find it helpful to speak this phrase whenever you detect an enemy tactic at work:

> Truly he is my rock and my salvation; he is my fortress, I shall never be shaken.
> PSALM 62:2

Talking it

- Which of the enemy's tactics are you most likely to be derailed by when you try to pray?
- Have you ever found yourself believing lies about yourself or others? How did it affect you, and what helped you to discover and believe the truth?
- We've talked about enemy tactics that might disrupt our personal prayer lives, but what enemy tactics do you see disrupting your church's prayer life?

Sustaining it

1 Raise a shield
One of the reasons military leaders like to know what ammunition their enemy is using is so they can provide their soldiers with the most appropriate defensive equipment. If you know the enemy uses a certain tactic on you, then get in ahead of him and raise a shield. If the tactic is busyness, for instance, book your prayer time into your diary and ask others to help you keep it, come what may. If the tactic is accusation, start your prayer time by reading some scripture verses

about how God sees you. If the tactic is disappointment with God, remind yourself that you're not yet at the end of the story.

2 Tend your relationships
Misunderstandings are fertile ground for us to start believing lies about each other. If there seems to be tension in a relationship, take time to meet the person and talk about it if you can. You'll be amazed at how that will liberate your praying later. If you can't resolve the tension here and now (and sometimes we can't), then hand it over to God each time you pray, so that it doesn't distract you.

3 Swap stories
When describing Satan as the accuser, the voice in John's vision also said that Satan would be overcome by testimony (Revelation 12:11). That basically means that as we tell each other about the good things God is doing for us, all the enemy's tactics lose their power. Do you have a story of something good that God has done for you recently? Why not find someone to tell it to? It will help both of you to overcome.

Victory strategies
Matthew 6:10; Luke 10:19; Acts 4:24–31; Ephesians 6:10–18; James 4:7

A month or so after that fateful day on the station when I noticed my retina had started to detach, I found myself scheduled for an operation to prevent any further damage. Despite my eyes being so complicated, one London hospital had recently acquired the equipment to treat eyes endoscopically (by putting cameras in on long needles), and that groundbreaking operation saved almost all the sight I still have. It isn't much, to be honest, but it matters to me, so I was overjoyed. The day before surgery, I was at home praying, and God drew my attention to a song by Godfrey Birtill, 'I will stand'. He told me to learn the lyrics, so I could sing them during my recovery from the operation. Since every other line of the song includes the song title, it wasn't difficult to do. I learnt it, and then promptly forgot all about it.

As I surfaced from the haze of general anaesthetic, the nurse said something about me having to lie on my left-hand side for two weeks. She assumed I knew already, but I didn't, and I was horrified. I had things I wanted to be getting on with, and I hadn't planned two weeks of horizontal convalescence. As I railed against the unfairness of it all, God gently reminded me of the song. Lying dutifully on my left side, I began to sing. By the third recurrence of 'I will stand', I was in fits of laughter. God had known I'd be prone for weeks, so he'd given me a song to sing about standing. Whatever opposition I'd encountered, and whatever position my body might be in, I was to spend those two weeks 'standing' in defiant prayer for our city and for the prayer week we were planning.

The early church knew more about opposition than most. No sooner had the Holy Spirit been poured out on them than they were being hauled before the authorities and told to be quiet. Acts 4:24–31 describes their response to opposition, and it is a masterclass for us in how to take ground, even when it feels like the enemy has too much power. Notice that their response to opposition was a prayer. That is where all spiritual warfare begins.

First and foremost, their prayer was a declaration of their intent to stand, despite what might come against them, and that is at the heart of spiritual warfare. In Paul's famous teaching on the armour of God (Ephesians 6:10–18), the command to stand appears no less than four times. We often think spiritual warfare involves some fancy footwork in prayer, knowing the right words to say and the best Bible verses to quote, but simple tenacity and determination are two of the deadliest weapons we possess. As the church declared its intent to stand, the Holy Spirit declared his intent to stand with them, by shaking the room (Acts 4:31). When we set our hearts, minds and wills to stand for what we know God has called us to do, the Holy Spirit joins his resolve to ours, and wonders start happening.

It's important to note that they stood together (Acts 4:24). As I 'stood' on my left side for two weeks, praying for transformation in our city, I was not alone. There were many others who were working towards our prayer week and who themselves were facing opposition. We stood together. God does not call you to stand alone. He has given you others to stand with you as you pray – even if you haven't met them yet.

Second, their prayer was mostly worship and the declaration of scripture (Acts 4:25–26). They knew that they would only find strength to stand in the battle if they bowed before God in worship. The apostle James would have been there on that day, and I often wonder if he was remembering that occasion when he penned his epistle years later.

> So then, surrender to God. Stand up to the devil and resist him
> and he will turn and run away from you.
> JAMES 4:7 (TPT)

If you've ever disliked someone intensely, then you'll know how unpleasant it is to be in a place where they are being praised. The same goes for every power and authority that opposes God's rule and reign: it withdraws when he is being worshipped. If you're feeling the heat of opposition, press into praise.

Finally, their prayer was a battle cry for mission (Acts 4:29–30). They didn't ask for protection (though there's nothing wrong with doing that); they didn't ask for God to deal with their enemies (though many in the Bible did pray for that); they prayed for boldness to go out and tell even more people about Jesus. Spiritual warfare is not about winning a battle against Satan – that was done by Jesus through a cross and an empty tomb. Spiritual warfare is about making sure everyone knows that the powers of darkness have been defeated, and that freedom, peace and lasting joy are available through Jesus Christ. Spiritual warfare starts in prayer, but it means nothing if it never gets any further. Your warfare prayers might be as stirring and eloquent as Churchillian war speeches, but if you never actually help anyone find hope in Jesus, then you haven't made a start on spiritual warfare.

> I have given you authority to trample on snakes and scorpions and to overcome all the power of the enemy; nothing will harm you.
> LUKE 10:19

These were the words Jesus greeted his disciples with, not when they returned from a prayer meeting but when they returned from a mission trip. Our prayers disarm the enemy and our worship drives him away, but we only overcome him completely when we help people to step from darkness into light.

We did eventually do that prayer week in Canterbury. After all we'd been through to get there, it was incredible to be able to open the door and see who God would bring us. Not 24 hours after we'd opened, we suddenly found a huge queue of people lining the street outside. Sadly they weren't headed our way – they were queueing for a light show at the cathedral a few doors down – but we were able to serve them drinks and tell them about our little prayer shop. Seeing the prayer room spill out on to the street in mission felt like the most natural thing in the world.

At the heart of all spiritual warfare is the phrase that is also at the heart of the prayer Jesus taught his disciples: 'your kingdom come, your will be done, on earth as it is in heaven' (Matthew 6:10).

Trying it

Opposition can feel both exhausting and intimidating, and that's when praise comes into its own. If you're feeling worn down, write a list of all the obstacles you're facing at the moment – everything that feels insurmountable and oppressive. Then go through your list again, writing one truth about God next to each obstacle. For example, if your list includes relationship tensions, you might write, 'Thank you, Jesus, that you are the Prince of Peace.' Then stand up and read your second list out loud as a prayer of praise.

Talking it

- Have you ever been in a situation where you've had to stand with others in prayer because you've come up against opposition? What was the situation, and what was the outcome?
- Thinking about Jesus' words to his disciples (Luke 10:19), how would you say the power of the enemy is being overcome in your local community?
- If spiritual warfare is as much about mission as prayer, how can we ensure that prayer and mission are woven tightly together in church life?

Sustaining it

1 Standing together
Is there something you're standing for in prayer at the moment? It's always better to stand together, so ask God to show you others who might be standing for the same thing. See if you can pray together, or at least keep in touch and share your insights.

2 Armour each other up
One of the benefits of fighting alongside others is that you always have people to watch your back and help you put your cumbersome armour on. You may have prayed through Ephesians 6:10–18 before, putting the armour on yourself, but have you got into a habit of praying that armour for your family, friends and church family? Standing together means looking out for one another and locking our shields together.

3 Don't stop at prayer
Does your rhythm of life include opportunities to help others to find Jesus? If not, open a space for mission. You could join a church

mission activity, or simply head to a coffee shop each week and chat to whoever you happen to meet there.

Group prayer activity

Is there something good happening in your community that is pushing back darkness? Talk together about how your group could join the battle by blessing that work in a practical way.

12

Resilience

There is not in the world a kind of life more sweet and delightful than that of a continual conversation with God; those only can comprehend it who practise and experience it.

Brother Lawrence, *The Practice of the Presence of God, and The Spiritual Maxims*
(Cosimo, 2006)

Building a rhythm
Matthew 6:9–13

I remember once reading about the flight habits of certain species of large birds. If you're particularly large, and you're built for a life of flying, beating gravity to lift your own body weight into the sky can be tricky. For birds like the bald eagle and the albatross, flying is a mixture of two essential processes: flapping and soaring. Flapping is, of course, using muscle-power to move their wings, propelling them through the sky; and soaring is using a thermal – a pocket of rising warm air – to lift them higher than they could ever fly with wing power alone.

That's a beautiful picture of prayer. Prayer doesn't just happen. It takes intentional spiritual muscle power on our part, choosing to prioritise it among the demands of the day, but it should never be purely a matter of flapping. The albatross who never finds a thermal soon ends up losing height and getting exhausted. If your prayer life feels like the frantic flapping of tired wings, then it may be because you need an updraught of the Holy Spirit. On the other hand, updraughts don't last forever, and the albatross that doesn't flap its wings is likely to end up back at sea level in no time at all. Having risen on the thermal, it has to start using its wings again, so that it keeps moving forwards and doesn't lose height. You and I need both types of prayer: the experiences that lift us, and the disciplines that keep us moving forwards. Only then do we have a rhythm of prayer that is resilient enough to withstand the winds and tides of life.

Jesus offered his disciples a timeless template for prayer (Matthew 6:9–13). Two thousand years after he first taught it to them, its verbal form is still used in churches across the world. But the Lord's Prayer, as it is often known, is far more of a rhythm than a prayer. It encompasses the key components of a healthy, resilient prayer life, and if you understand those components, and understand a little about yourself, it is possible to build that rhythm into your life in a way that works and lasts. It won't all be exhilarating updraughts, but neither will it all be weary flapping. It will be the day-to-day communion with God that is uniquely perfect for you.

Jesus' template begins with what are probably the most famous words of prayer:

> Our Father in heaven, hallowed be your name.
> MATTHEW 6:9

Before anything else, the prayer relationship between you and God is about being present to each other. He is always with you, and you probably chat to him as you go through the day, but like any relationship, prayer needs to include time spent face-to-face, rather than just walking side by side through life. And that face-to-face encounter really should be an updraught experience. There may well be difficult conversations to be had, there may be work to be done together, but the moment of turning your gaze on the Father who loves you beyond all measure should be an exhilarating, soul-lifting moment.

Here's where knowing yourself helps immensely. Not everyone finds that moment of face-to-face encounter in the same way. If you are an introvert or a contemplative, there's a strong chance you'll find it easiest to connect with God when you're alone, perhaps through the practices of stillness or scripture meditation. If you're an extrovert or an activist, on the other hand, being alone and still may be the least helpful way to connect with the Father. For you, being outside, being with other people or praying in an active way may prove far more helpful in sensing God's presence and drawing near to him. If you're someone who's energised by taking care of people or making the world a kinder place, then you might find it easiest to draw near to the Father if you're bringing him someone or something you care about deeply. As you carry the situation to him in intercession, so you find yourself in that face-to-face encounter with him. If you're someone who loves intellectual stimulation, you may find that some thought-provoking reading is the best way to encounter him. If you're a thinker, then your intellect is the landing strip for the Holy Spirit, so in-depth thought will cause you to become more aware of him.

And those are just a few suggestions. In time, of course, you'll be able to catch the updraught of his presence in a hundred different ways, but the best place to start is to find the way that best suits your personality. As you try out the exercises in this book, you'll hopefully get a feel for which types of prayer bring you most alive to his presence.

Once you're face-to-face, the immediate response is worship. Even as we draw near, we 'hallow' his name – we celebrate his character and his ways. It's easy to get stuck in a narrow view of worship, assuming it must involve singing songs and forming impressive theological soliloquys, but worship is richer when you allow your personality to shine through. Most parents would choose a home-made birthday card from their children over a shop-bought one any day. How much more, then, must your Father in heaven love it when you celebrate him in a way that's wholly you? As you call to mind his astonishing goodness, what does it make you want to do in response? That's the best place to start your worship.

The second component of Jesus' template for prayer is intercession.

> Your kingdom come, your will be done, on earth as it is in heaven.
> MATTHEW 6:10

No sooner have we looked into the face of the Father than he turns our gaze outwards to the world that so badly needs him. No rhythm of prayer is ever complete when it only concerns us and our issues. We are given the gift of prayer that we might use it to unleash blessing on the world around us. And each of us has a circle of people and situations we get to bless. Yours may include family, friends, neighbours and work colleagues, but it may also include organisations whose work you see as particularly important, or causes God has put on your heart. Who is in your circle of blessing? Who has God given you to pray for?

There are many different ways to do this kind of praying, and your personality will determine which you choose. You may find you bless by using words to pray for people, or you may prefer expressing your prayers through practical actions. You might like to pray instinctively and spontaneously, or you might prefer to devise a prayer strategy to help you cover topics more thoroughly. And, of course, your personality will influence whether you prefer to do this kind of prayer alone or with others. Whichever method you choose, this component of your prayer rhythm should feel like a muscle-stretching flap of the wings. That doesn't mean it's not enjoyable or inspiring; it just means it's the kind of prayer where you work hard in partnership with God to see his kingdom come.

The third component of Jesus' prayer strategy turned his disciples' attention back to themselves, their physical needs and their emotional well-being:

Give us today our daily bread. And forgive us our debts, as we also have forgiven our debtors.
MATTHEW 6:11–12

If you've ever wondered whether praying for yourself is selfish, then notice that these two sentences take up a significant chunk of the prayer. Prayer is the place where we draw nourishment from God. We bring our needs and we draw on his provision; we bring our failures and we draw on his grace; we bring our brokenness and we draw on his healing. These aren't things we do once in a while when we get desperate; they're things we need to do regularly. That's why they're part of Jesus' template.

To return to the albatross analogy, this is another area of prayer that should feel more like soaring than flapping. It's not that it's easy – things like forgiveness are often hard-won – but even if you're the kind of person who doesn't much enjoy introspection, this kind of prayer should be a moment when you experience God's love restoring you and his power renewing you. If the first component of this template for prayer is about being face-to-face with the Father, then this component is about leaning into his strength and feeling his embrace. It is where our frailty meets his might, where his tenderness meets our pain. As such, it's the journey of knowing more of him and more of ourselves.

Depending on your personality, you'll either engage with this kind of prayer more easily by thinking it or by feeling it. If you're the thinking type, then you may find that reading, studying and analysing are good ways to know more of God and of yourself: mining the scriptures for treasures you've never spotted before; journalling about your own journey with God; and using exercises like the Ignatian Examen to help you reflect on what God might be doing in your life (see the end of Chapter 1). If prayer is more about feelings for you, you will probably prefer practices that engage your emotions: listening to music; soaking in scriptures that bring God's character to life for you; noticing the feelings that stir in you as you pray; pouring out your heart in an unstructured flow; and using your body to accentuate your words. Remember, there's no right or wrong way to do these things, as long as you are getting to know God more and becoming more alert to his work in your life.

The final component of Jesus' template for prayer was a reminder of the battle that always ensues when the kingdom of God is established:

> And lead us not into temptation, but deliver us from the
> evil one.
> MATTHEW 6:13

For many of us, the only time we mention anything to do with the enemy in prayer is when we say this line, yet dealing with the reality of warfare should be a regular part of our prayer rhythm. If you ask someone to deliver you, it implies that you believe in the destructive power of whatever you need delivering from. If you accept the reality of its destructive power, then it follows that you want to be involved in seeing the effects of that power diminish – and that happens through prayer.

But prayer that wages war on the darkness in our world doesn't have to be warrior-like. You may be the type who enjoys a lot of noise and movement in prayer, in which case your approach to this kind of prayer will be bold, vocal and energetic; but wars are fought as much by intelligence-gathering and codebreaking as by firing weapons. Perhaps your 'deliver us from evil' prayer will be more about doing some research to understand the impact of child poverty in your local community, and then praying about the trigger factors that are exacerbating it. Or perhaps your 'lead us not into temptation' prayer will be to visit someone who's living in the grip of addiction. There are as many ways to push back the frontiers of darkness in this world as there are people who pray, and your way will be different to everyone else's.

The Lord's Prayer isn't a ritual to be performed; it's a rhythm to be lived. If you can spend a little time in each of the four components once a week, it's a good start. It's better to start small and move slowly than to set yourself an impossibly high standard that you never achieve. And throughout it all, remember that he made you just the way you are. He doesn't want you to emulate someone else's prayer rhythm or match someone else's pace. He simply wants to remain in you, and you in him.

Trying it

Which of the four components in Jesus' prayer template do you practise least? Make space to try it out in the next few days, but be sure to use a style of prayer that suits your personality.

Talking it

- Why do you think the church has continued to use the Lord's Prayer so faithfully for so many years? What do you think is the value of using it in corporate worship?
- Do you pray in ways that reflect your personality? If so, what do you do?
- Prayer in church can lack variety at times, and it often suits one personality type more than others. How can we vary the way we pray together so that our corporate prayer reflects our diverse personalities?

Sustaining it

1 Say the Lord's Prayer daily

Praying the Lord's Prayer is a good way of reminding yourself of those four components, but it's also a good way of making sure you stop once a day for a moment of prayer. Set an alarm on your watch or phone, and wherever you are when the alarm sounds, stop and pray the prayer Jesus taught his disciples.

2 Use a structure
If you find structure helpful, then there are several templates around that you can use to structure your daily prayer time. You could use the Lord's Prayer, for instance, spending a few minutes on each of the four components; you could use ACTS (adoration, confession, thanksgiving and supplication); or you could use the various elements of the Jerusalem temple. This kind of structured approach doesn't suit everyone, but it may be just what you need to get your rhythm started.

3 Get to know yourself
There are plenty of resources out there to help you discover more about your personality type and how it might shape the way you pray. Take some time to explore and learn. It can be both enriching and liberating.

Growing a relationship
Jeremiah 31:33–34; John 15:5–8

I was sitting on a stage in front of a church full of people, talking about the book I'd just had published. The book was all about faith, and in one of the chapters I had talked a little about my experiences of having unsuccessful IVF treatment. The interviewer invited me to read an excerpt, and as I finished, he asked me that devastatingly simple question, 'So, what's the point of praying if it doesn't always work?'

We had agreed the questions in advance, and I knew that his direct delivery was meant to engage the audience in the subject of prayer, but for a few seconds it caught me unawares. What actually was the point? I spend my life telling people prayer is important and powerful, but what kind of an advert am I when my life contains such huge unanswered prayers? In that tightrope moment, I opened my mouth, and as the words came out, I realised they were from the deepest, truest part of me. I replied, 'God may not always give me what I've asked for, but he always gives me himself, and that is worth every bit of praying I could ever do.'

Prayer may well have power to liberate, restore and transform, but that's not the point of it at all. Prayer is a relationship with God himself. When the Israelites were going around in circles of fear and disobedience, God sent prophets to speak to them about what that relationship would look like, and one of the phrases he used many times was, 'I will be their God, and they will be my people' (Jeremiah 31:33). It was not, 'They will do things for me, and in return I'll do things for them.'

It's all too easy to get into the habit of seeing prayer as transactional: if we do the right things by God, then he'll deliver in response to our requests. So much of life feels like that, and if we're honest many of our human relationships work that way, even if we don't mean them to. But nothing could be further from God's heart. He offers us unconditional love and unbreakable communion. All we have to do is choose it by choosing Jesus.

> I am the sprouting vine and you're my branches. As you live in union with me as your source, fruitfulness will stream from within you – but when you live separated from me you are powerless.
>
> JOHN 15:5 (TPT)

Prayer is the relationship of belonging: he is your God and you belong to him. Prayer is the life-union that Jesus was describing when he used that beautiful image of the vine. Prayer is the fusing together of you and God. That fusing may bring forth all sorts of good things for you and those around you, but that's really all bonus. What prayer brings is the endless, unstoppable flow of God's life into yours, by his Spirit.

I remember the day I took the call to say that our final IVF cycle had failed. I knew it was the end of that four-year story, and by rights

I should have felt empty and devastated. As I ended the call, I did feel the beginnings of suffocating grief, but I could also feel something else – an inexplicable sense of hope. It wasn't the kind of concrete hope you get when you're looking forward to something; it was more like a strong, wild sense that this was only the beginning of something new. And I was swirled around by those conflicting feelings for years. The grief was real. It ran its course as all grief should. But the hope was just as real. It would bubble up in me at the strangest of times, making me want to run for the future ahead of me.

Over the years, people have commented that I must be a resilient person to survive that painful experience, but what's resilient is my life-union with God in prayer. It doesn't mean I've had a brilliant prayer rhythm, or that I've always followed the template of prayer we were looking at in the first half of this chapter. I need to read this book as much as anyone. It just means that I have known what it is to be fused with God at the deepest level, to receive his life, to draw on his strength and to feel the wildfire of his Spirit. Every time a prayer hasn't been answered, he's been there. Every time disappointment has threatened to overwhelm me, he's been there. I may have retreated from him at times, but he has never retreated from me.

This book is packed with prayer activities, but I sincerely hope you never think that prayer activities are what will keep you connected to God. You are joined with him – a branch of his vine – and that is a fact. The trouble with us branches is that we all too often forget the life flowing through us and look for alternative sources of life. If a prayer rhythm does anything, it helps us to stop long enough to notice the life already flowing in us by God's Spirit. It steadies us and focuses us, so that we draw from him, rather than relying on other things to sustain us.

> 'No longer will they teach their neighbour, or say to one another, "Know the Lord," because they will all know me, from the least of them to the greatest,' declares the Lord.
> JEREMIAH 31:34

God wants you to know him. Of course, it delights his heart if you love him, please him, praise him and serve him, but at the heart of it all is his longing that you should know him. Knowing him isn't obligatory, but it is unimaginably beautiful. Knowing him won't make him love you more – he already loves you infinitely – but it will tune your heart to feel the joy of that love. It won't make all your problems go away, but it will help you see them differently. It won't guarantee you health or wealth, popularity or status, but it will set your soul ablaze.

And there is only one way to know God, and that is prayer.

Trying it

Getting to know God may take years, but it can start today. Before you begin this exercise, ask God to teach you something new about himself. Then choose either Jeremiah 31:33–34 or John 15:5–8, and read it aloud slowly. Then read it again, this time in your head, and ask God to make a word or phrase stand out to you. When something catches your attention, stop reading (even if you haven't got to the end) and simply meditate on the word or phrase that struck you. What does it tell you about God?

Talking it

- Have you ever known a time when disappointment, anger or grief have blocked your way to God?
- When you think about a branch growing on a vine, what does it tell you about what prayer should and shouldn't be like?
- What's the most helpful thing you've learnt about God as you've worked through this book?

Sustaining it

1 Contemplate a plant

One of the best ways to understand what it means to be a branch on a vine is to look long and hard at a plant. Make it a daily practice for the next week to look at a plant that's growing, and to meditate on what you see.

2 Dig out disappointment

Disappointment can be toxic, both to your mental health and to your prayer life. If you are finding it hard to recover from disappointment at an unanswered prayer, tell someone you trust and ask them to pray for you. Having a friend who knows can be a great comfort.

3 Make yourself accountable

If you're keen to build more of a rhythm of prayer in your life, find someone else who's keen to do the same and check in with each other regularly, sharing what you've done and helping each other to think of prayer practices that might suit your personalities. If they haven't read this book, you could buy them a copy and work through it together.

Group prayer activity

The best way to reflect on vines and branches is to go where things are growing. Take your group for a walk in a place of natural beauty, and talk and pray together about what it means to grow in relationship with Jesus.

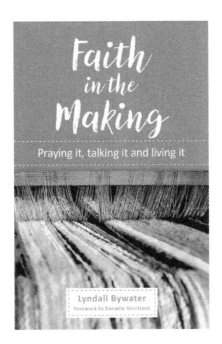

If faith is 'being sure of what we hope for and certain of what we do not see', what does that look like in practice today? In a world that is largely unsure and uncertain, how do we gain our confidence? *Faith in the Making* recognises the problem and seeks the answer in the list of faithful heroes found in Hebrews 11. This accessible devotional resource will inspire individuals and groups to live more confidently for God in today's world. Heroic faith is far more attainable than we often think!

Faith in the Making
Praying it, talking it and living it
Lyndall Bywater
978 0 85746 555 9 £7.99

brfonline.org.uk

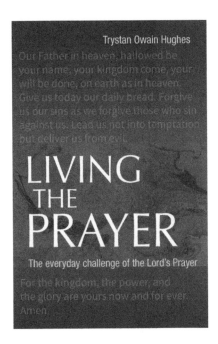

What are we really saying when we say the Lord's Prayer? What are we expecting? *Living the Prayer* is a fresh perspective on the Lord's Prayer. Rooted in the Bible as well as in contemporary culture, it explores how this prayer can radically challenge and transform our daily lives. Contained in the prayer's 63 words is a fresh and innovative way of viewing, and acting in, the world that is as relevant now as it was 2,000 years ago. The author shows that this revolutionary prayer demands that we don't remain on our knees, but rather that we work towards making God's topsy-turvy, downside-up kingdom an everyday reality.

Living the Prayer
The everyday challenge of the Lord's Prayer
Trystan Owain Hughes
978 0 85746 623 5 £7.99

brfonline.org.uk

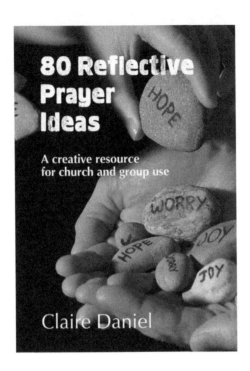

Prayer remains a vital part of Christian discipleship. Following the success of the author's *80 Creative Prayer Ideas*, this ready-to-use resource book contains 80 further ideas on setting up reflective and creative prayer stations or responses. Claire Daniel shows us how to pray with our whole being – our senses as well as our voice, our hearts as much as our minds. Tried and tested, these ideas will enhance the praying of small groups, churches and individuals.

80 Reflective Prayer Ideas
A creative resource for church and group use
Claire Daniel
978 0 85746 673 0 £9.99

brfonline.org.uk

Transforming
lives and communities

Christian growth and understanding of the Bible

Resourcing individuals, groups and leaders in churches for their own spiritual journey and for their ministry

Church outreach in the local community

Offering two programmes that churches are embracing to great effect as they seek to engage with their local communities and transform lives

Teaching Christianity in primary schools

Working with children and teachers to explore Christianity creatively and confidently

Children's and family ministry

Working with churches and families to explore Christianity creatively and bring the Bible alive

parenting for faith

Visit **brf.org.uk** for more information on BRF's work

brf.org.uk

The Bible Reading Fellowship (BRF) is a Registered Charity (No. 233280)